Religion and Nationalism in Soviet Ukraine after 1945

The Millennium Series

Religion and Nationalism in Soviet Ukraine after 1945

Vasyl Markus

Ukrainian Studies Fund
Harvard University
Cambridge, Massachusetts

Printed in the United States of America

The Ukrainian Studies Fund, Inc. was established in 1957. Its purpose is to raise funds for the establishment and support of Ukrainian scholarly centers at American universities. The organization has endowed three chairs in Ukrainian studies (history, literature, and linguistics) at Harvard University, and is in the process of completing the endowment of Harvard's Ukrainian Research Institute.

The Friends of HURI was established by a group of young professionals concerned about the cultural development of Ukraine and committed to the advancement of Ukrainian scholarship. The founding principle of this organization was two-fold: to seek financial support for HURI in the Ukrainian community and to draw the community into the academic and social life of Harvard University.

A generous subsidy toward the publication of this booklet has been provided by Katherina Kotowycz, Chrystyna Blazenko, Paraskewia Pikas Wytwycka, and Maria M. Ovchynnyk, outstanding contributors to the Ukrainian Studies Fund at Harvard University.

CONTENTS

FOREWORD

In 1988 Ukrainians throughout the world will celebrate the Millennium of the Christianization of Rus'-Ukraine. An important part of these observances will be the promotion of scholarly inquiry into the process of Christianization and the thousand-year Christian Ukrainian spiritual and cultural tradition. The Ukrainian Research Institute of Harvard University proposes to undertake a number of projects, including sponsorship of an international scholarly conference, the publication of a multi-volume source series and a comprehensive history of the Ukrainian Church, and the establishment of a chair devoted to the religious history of Ukraine at the Harvard Divinity School. In addition to providing financial assistance to the Institute for the realization of these plans, the Ukrainian Studies Fund has established a position at Keston College, Kent, the United Kingdom for a Ukrainian researcher whose purpose is to examine the present status of religion in Ukraine. In cooperation with the Friends of the Harvard Ukrainian Research Institute, the Fund has also initiated the Millennium Series of seminal studies on topics of Ukrainian religious and cultural history.

Religion, church and ecclesiastical institutions have always exerted an enormous influence on Ukrainian political affairs and national culture. In two articles reprinted here, Professor Vasyl Markus of Loyola University investigates the relationship between religion and nation in contemporary Ukraine. In "Religion and Nationalism in Ukraine," he provides an analytical framework for examining the faiths (Orthodox, Catholic, Protestant, Jewish, Muslim) and national identity (Ukrainian, Russian, Polish, Hungarian, Jewish) in the Ukrainian SSR. He pays particular attention to the conflict between the upholders of Ukrainian nationalism, the Ukrainian Autocephalous Orthodox Church and the Ukrainian Catholic Church, on the one hand and the upholder of Russian nationalism and Russian/Soviet imperialism, the Russian Orthodox Church, on the other. In his article, "Religion and Nationality: The Uniates of the Ukraine," Professor Markus demonstrates that the link between Ukrainian national culture and the Ukrainian Catholic religious tradition has not been broken in the Western Ukraine despite the forcible liquidation of the Church by Soviet authorities forty years ago. The articles provide a deeper understanding of why Soviet treatment of religious groups must be examined in the light of long-term historical factors and in the context of Soviet nationality policies whose ultimate aim is Russification.

Professor Vasyl Markus teaches international relations, Soviet politics, and international law at Loyola University. He also is the associate editor of *The Encyclopedia of the Ukraine*, published by the University of Toronto Press.

Harvard Ukrainian Studies Fund
Cambridge, Massachusetts

Religion and Nationalism in Ukraine

The Soviet sociopolitical landscape of the present day Ukraine has been shaped by forces and an ideology that deny both the religious value system and the national aspirations of the Ukrainian people. In the view of the architects of this social engineering, religion as a state of mind and its institutionalized expression, the church, should have yielded to a new enlightened Weltanschauung: scientific communism, embracing also atheism. In spite of massive efforts on the part of the political establishment, the process of substitution of a secular religion for a revealed one has had limited success. Similarly, nationalism, allegedly a product of class antagonisms in presocialist society, has maintained its vitality and constitutes a formidable challenge to the supranational Soviet Russian societal model.

Moreover, religion and nationalism, labeled reactionary vis-à-vis the "progressive" new social and international order that the communist party of the Soviet Union intends to shape, have succeeded in forging an alliance against their common enemy. This might be viewed as a simple expediency, a tactical maneuver in the face of a common threat. Yet a closer historical investigation and cultural-psychological analysis of the two phenomena will attest to an interdependence and, at times, to a symbiosis of religious and national ideas. Judaism is certainly a prototype of such a coalescence of the religious and the secular. Christianity, although a universalist religion with a new message according to which "there is no room for distinction between Greek and Jew, between the circumcised and the uncircumcised, or between barbarian and Scythian, slave and free man" (Col. 3:11), was not immune to the nationalist contamination. Certainly, Western Christianity succeeded for a while in creating a multinational empire in the form of the Holy Roman Empire of the German nation. But the empire succumbed to new ideas and to forces generated within the same Christianity in its pristine reformist incarnation. Likewise, Eastern Byzantine Christianity attempted to construct its own supranational model, although with even less success. Particular national-cultural entities soon emerged and threatened the ideals of the universal Byzantine Empire, as later they would challenge Islam.

Church and religion often have been articulators and supporters of imperial universal designs. But within the same church, and among adherents of the same religion, movements have emerged to hinder such designs in the name of national self-assertion and cultural self-actualization. Eastern Europe and the orbit of the Third Rome served as another example of the perplexing interplay between religion and nationalism, church and public power. In certain periods some church organizations and religious leaders have supported larger political structures with one nation in a privileged position while other Christians, Orthodox or Catholic, fought against such structures and articulated rival national ideologies. In most cases, among the ruling and the ruled national entities, we find a coalescence between religion and nationalism. A tendency toward a closer relationship between them within the same society is prevalent when both, or just one of them, are threatened from the outside.

The Ukrainian case concerning the nationality-religion relationship demonstrates some similarities with, and differences from, analogous cases in Eastern Europe, e.g., the Polish, Russian, Lithuanian, and Romanian cases. In periods of Ukrainian political autonomy, the institutionalized religion tended to support secular power and vice versa (Kievan Rus', the Ukrainian Cossack state). At times when Ukraine was deprived of its independence, as has been the case throughout most of its history, the church either remained a catalyst of the national consciousness (and its last refuge), or was forced, even manipulated, into being an instrument of assimilation with foreign ruling nations and serving their interests in Ukraine.

Potentially an assimilative role could have been assigned to the Uniate church by the Polish sponsors of the Union of Brest (1596), which brought Ukrainians and Belorussians under the authority of Roman pontiffs. Yet there were strong forces operating within that church, as well as outside it—mainly among the non-Uniate branch of the Church of Rus'—which molded it into an expression of Ukrainian (Ruthenian) nationhood.[1] There were periods and situations when some segments of that church served as mediators of a supranational Polish ideology. This has been expressed in acceptance of the imperial-feudal national identification (*natione Polonus, gente Ruthenus*) and in close rapprochement with, if not in the absorption into, Roman Catholicism. The latter, theoretically, was universal and non-national. In reality it was imbued with Polish culture and national pride. This Polish option of the Brest Union materialized only partly, scoring individual successes in absorbing some members of the Ukrainian political elite or, exceptionally, in bringing over to Polish Catholicism a few hundred thousand people, as in the Cholm region. The Uniate church, as a whole, did not prove just an ephemeral creature and instrument of conversion (or transmission); it had developed into a Ukrainian national institution and has remained so to the present day.

It was the strongly anti-Catholic Orthodox church in Ukraine that restored its hierarchy in 1620 under the authority of Constantinople, that remained for over a century a more dynamic articulator of national aspirations. However, common religious bonds with Russian Orthodoxy and incorporation of the Ukrainian church into the patriarchate of Moscow in 1686, basically a political act, brought about the neutralization of Ukrainian Orthodoxy's national character and function. It was this neutralization that became a real menace to the Ukraine's national existence. Throughout the eighteenth century, Russian ecclesiastical and political authorities succeeded in enlisting the services of the Ukrainian hierarchy and clergy in pacifying autonomist currents. This was achieved by co-opting the human resources and absorbing the cultural values of the Kievan Orthodox heritage in the name of a higher "Pan-Russian" unity. Subsequently it brought about an accelerated Russification and integration of the Ukrainian church of the former Kiev Metropolia into the Russian church.

The nineteenth century witnessed almost a complete alienation of the Russianized Ukrainian clergy from the emerging modern national movement in Eastern Ukraine. Unlike other European societies, none of the ecclesiastical figures is known to have been active in the process of national revival in Eastern Ukraine. (In Bukovina, which was under Austrian domination, a few Orthodox priests did participate in it, however.) In contrast, the Galician (West Ukrainian) revival largely was promoted and led by the Uniate clergy. But some clerics there—particularly in Hungarian Transcarpathia—partly due to foreign influence and partly in reaction to menacing Polish and Hungarian nationalism, looked to Russia as the "protector of the Slavs" and promoted the Russification of local Ukrainians ("Little Russians" or "Carpathorussians"). Even in that capacity, representatives of the church served as agents of nationalism—in this case, Russian nationalism. The so-called Russophile (*Moskvofily*) movement among Western Ukrainians in the nineteenth and twentieth centuries collided with the dynamic, popular Ukrainian nationalism and plainly lost this historic cultural and political confrontation. The religious dimension of this struggle made itself evident through the support given to the Russophiles by the Russian church and the Synod, as well as by the fact that the Uniate church and, later, the Ukrainian autocephaly, constituted the spiritual backbone of the secular national movement.[2]

Early in the twentieth century and during the Revolution of 1917–1920, in the Russian-ruled Ukraine only a minority of the lower-rank clergy embraced the Ukrainian national cause. Slowly, they came to realize that Ukraine, if it was to survive as an independent nation, needed a separate church organization and its own religious ideology. This brought about the movement to create an autocephalous Ukrainian Orthodox church. Autocephalists invoked the period of relative autonomy and the traditions of the Kievan church under Metropolitan Petro Mohyla and his successors prior to 1686 as their frame of reference. Ukrainian autocephaly also was inspired by the democratic and popular nature of the Ukrainian liberation movement during the revolution that culminated in the establishment of the Ukrainian National Republic.[3]

The autocephalous church has been, in its substance, politically nationalist, and ideologically anti-Russian and anti-authoritarian, while the Russian church remained Russian nationalist and imperial. The Russian Patriarchal church acted on the Ukrainian territory through the native Ukrainian and Russian clerics or laymen who abhorred the nationalist inspirations of the autocephalists, without admitting Russian nationalist motivations in their own stand. Certainly, those nationalisms were diverse in form and in certain expressions but the same in substance. Thus, two trends in the Orthodox religion in Ukraine existed side-by-side, often indulging in conflict and mutual recriminations inspired by hostile nationalisms, viz., a separatist (Ukrainian) and integrationist (Russian) organization. The latter was, under certain circumstances, willing to admit an autonomous (as opposed to autocephalous) status for the Orthodox church in Ukraine

The Ukrainian Autocephalous Orthodox church, formally established in 1921 was initially tolerated by the Soviet regime, even viewed for a while as a more "progressive" force in opposition to the "reactionary" Russian Orthodox church It soon established itself in the Soviet Ukraine not only as a protector of the Ukrainian Orthodox people against the authoritarian and monarchist church of Moscow, but also as a stronghold of national aspirations when Ukrainian separatist nationalism failed to prevail over Soviet power. Many former political activists joined the ranks and even the leadership of the Autocephalous church, which was becoming increasingly popular. As a result, the church was attacked by the party and by the Soviet government, which saw in it a real danger to the multinational Soviet state. In 1930, the Autocephalous church was suppressed and its leadership decimated. It was not accidental that a major show trial in 1929–30 against the Union of the Liberation of Ukraine implicated also the leadership of the Autocephalous church.[4]

The Uniates or the Ukrainian Catholic Church of the Eastern Rite, which before 1944 acted outside Soviet control, played an even larger role in the modern national movement. The towering figure of the Metropolitan Andrei Sheptytsky, who for forty years headed the see of Lviv, personified the close relationship between the religious life and the national aspirations of Western Ukrainians. The government of the short-lived autonomous state of Carpatho-Ukraine (1938–39) was led by a Uniate priest, Msgr. Avhustyn Voloshyn. The Soviet regime, which took these territories under its rule in 1944–45 in a new historical effort to "collect all Russian lands," moved naturally against the Uniate church. Between 1946 and 1949, it was outlawed and cruelly suppressed in what was not so much a drive against religion as such, but one against a church that fostered a nationalism hostile to the regime.

Lacking only the formal act of dissolution, the same fate befell the Ukrainian Orthodox Autocephalous church, which had been restored on German-occupied territory during World War II. During the two or three years of relative religious freedom under the Germans, the idea of an autocephalous Ukrainian church had rallied a significant following among Soviet Ukrainians, thus becoming an important channel for revived Ukrainian nationalism. It was logical for Stalin to move against both national Ukrainian churches and to favor their absorption into the Russian Orthodox church. The latter succored the new Russian nationalism revived during World War II by the Kremlin in its search for legitimation. With the changed nationality and religious policies of the CPSU, Soviet leaders have preferred a conservative and nationalist Russian church in Ukraine to the local, autonomous national churches, because the latter proved themselves to be potent instruments of Ukrainian consciousness.

Present Status of Religion and Nationalism in Ukraine

Today's Ukraine is divided vaguely into two camps in terms of religion: those who believe and those who do not. It is difficult to assess numerically the two constituencies, yet, on the basis of sundry claims, one may infer that probably about half of the Ukrainian population still considers itself religious in the broadest sense. Most of the rest are flatly indifferent, ignorant, religiously passive, or intellectually areligious, but not necessarily militantly atheistic or antireligious. Only a slight minority of nonreligious individuals profess antireligious zeal and commitment to combat religion as a hostile ideology, though this is the main concern of those institutions of the system that specialize in antireligious propaganda. In Ukraine, as in other Soviet-ruled territories, only the high priests of secular atheism and their salaried lower rank preachers are truly antireligious.

Despite massive effort and tremendous financial input into antireligious work, religious communities in Ukraine have survived and are thriving. Soviet antireligious workers have to face in some way the issue of nationalism that does affect, although sometimes marginally, the sociopolitical life of the present-day Ukrainian society.

I have broken down the religious communities in Ukraine into four categories:

1. religious entities controlled by the regime, but enjoying some preferential treatment due to political expediency;
2. controlled and relatively restricted organizations;
3. organizations controlled with excessive restrictions;
4. organizations that are banned and openly persecuted.[5]

The Soviet totalitarian system does not recognize the autonomous existence of any religious body. Thus, the classic principle of the liberal church-state separation is not valid in the USSR; there the state is not neutral. Religion is not autonomous, but subject to control and manipulation for political purpose by those in power.

Preferentially Treated Religious Groups

The Russian Orthodox church is the only member of category one in Ukraine. Although the CPSU and the Soviet state are committed to the objectives of scientific communism, including the promotion of atheism, the Russian Orthodox church has, nevertheless, occupied a somewhat special place among religious bodies of the USSR since World War II. Having discovered that the Russian people were not giving up their ancestral religion, but had preserved it despite years of severe persecutions, and having realized that religion could strengthen the patriotic feeling of the masses, Stalin decided to stage a reconciliation with the church and its hierarchy. Instead of combating the church, he used it, particularly in those areas that were in the Russian Orthodox church's historic sphere of influence, and where non-Russian nationalism operated, actively or latently. In this regard, Ukraine was a primary target.

The first task of the Russian Orthodox church in Ukraine was to absorb the Ukrainian Autocephalous parishes and clergy which had been restored for a short time in the period 1941–44. Soviet authorities were opposed adamantly to the continuation of the *petlurite* church [6] that had emerged again under German auspices. The latter fact certainly was a serious liability, even though the church's promoters were no more pro-German than were their counterparts in the "autonomous" Orthodox church who supported unity with the Moscow patriarchate. The de facto suppression of Ukrainian autocephaly, without any formal act or pronouncement, was facilitated further by the mass exodus of that church's hierarchy and of the most outspoken clergy. The patriarchate and the government had to deal with only the lower echelons of clergy who reluctantly accepted the new state of affairs, tacitly joining the ranks of the Russian Orthodox church.

A more serious issue was the Russian Orthodox church's successful "reunification" of Ukrainian Catholicism with the see of the Moscow patriarchate. Despite a long and difficult struggle, the Russian Orthodox church and the Soviet regime eventually were able to sever local ties with Rome. The Russian church easily extracted concessions from the regime, in payment for its role in the pacification of Western Ukraine. The perseverance of nationalism in Ukraine and its continued identification with the Uniate church are the guarantee of the continued usefulness of the Russian Orthodox church in Ukraine to the regime.

For the Moscow patriarchate, the benefits are encouraging. The territory of the Ukraine, and particularly Western Ukraine, is one of the most religiously active parts of the USSR. There are about 2,500 parishes operating in the Ukrainian SSR, representing roughly one-third of all the parishes of the Moscow patriarchate. The number of eparchies is 18, with 15 bishops (out of a total of 76 in the USSR in 1978).[7] About 60 percent of the Ukrainian congregations are located in five West Ukrainian eparchies, underscoring their importance in the total structure of the Russian Orthodox church. With the exception of Lithuania and possibly Moldavia, the percentage of individuals practicing religion here is the highest in the USSR.

This does not mean that atheist work is not carried on in Western Ukraine or that church activities are not hindered. Some churches have been closed, registered priests are restrained and closely monitored, and bishops and other ranking church officials, being a part of quasi-*nomenklatura* appointments, are regulated thoroughly in their administrative activities and church personnel policies. But as long as there are other, more immediate targets—the tolerated, but socially dangerous, sectarian religious groups or politically "obnoxious" facts or people to be neutralized—a conservative and conventional religious community tends to become politically acceptable to the regime.

The marriage of convenience of Russian Orthodoxy in Ukraine with the system has, however, imposed a certain price. The very fact that the church initially embraced over 2,500 Uniate parishes and close to 1,500 Uniate priests, manifested itself in a new ethnic composition of the Orthodox church in Ukraine. The Ukrainian identity of the former Uniates, now forced into conversion to Orthodoxy, did not disappear. It remains visibly present and has to be tolerated. The language used in the liturgical functions is a Ukrainianized variant of Old Church Slavonic; the language of the sermons and of local administration is standard Ukrainian. Most of the local bishops are natives of Western Ukraine and 95 percent of the clergy consist of local people. A number of West Ukrainian rituals and ceremonies, different from those practiced elsewhere by the Russian Orthodox church, are tolerated.

In the 1950s, the Moscow patriarchate attempted to "orthodoxize" the newly attached congregations by eliminating the so-called Latinizing influences. In this respect, several measures were introduced vis-à-vis West Ukrainian clergy with few results.[8] The question of language, as the primary indicator of national perseverance, still remains crucial. When Metropolitan Filaret Denysenko, the patriarchal exarch of Ukraine, visits Western Ukraine, he addresses local congregations in Ukrainian. *Pravoslavnyi Visnyk* (one of the two Orthodox monthlies in the USSR) appears in Ukrainian. It also services substantially Russianized eparchies and parishes of central and eastern Ukraine. The only prayer book published in the Ukrainian SSR since World War II features Old Church Slavonic texts in the Ukrainian variant, together with some prayers in the Ukrainian vernacular.

An excessive zeal about Ukrainian language is viewed with suspicion. According to a *samvydav* source, a certain priest, Father Sava, started to preach in Kiev's St. Vladimir Cathedral in Ukrainian.[9] He was removed shortly thereafter and sent to a village church. The use of the Ukrainian language in the cathedral in the capital of Ukraine appears to have been more than regime officials and representatives of the Moscow patriarchate could stomach.

Nevertheless, the status of the church in Ukraine clearly was upgraded. Although not an autonomous branch of the patriarchate, the Ukrainian eparchies constitute an exarchate, the only one within the Russian Orthodox church in the Soviet Union. This might be due to the traditional prestige of the Metropolitan See of ancient Kiev. The present exarch, Metropolitan Filaret, enjoys a particular position within the Russian Orthodox hierarchy. He is second in rank to Patriarch Pimen and often represents the Russian Orthodox church and the Moscow patriarchate on ecumenical and foreign missions. The role of Filaret and of the exarchate was underscored when, in 1969, a department for the external relations of the Russian Orthodox church was established in Kiev.[10] This measure pursues a long-range objective, especially in dealing with the issues of the Ukrainian Catholic and Autocephalous Orthodox churches active in the diaspora.

Relatively Restricted Religious Groups

Among the churches in Ukraine that are tolerated and controlled, but not excessively restricted, are the Evangelical Christian-Baptists, the Reformed Church of Transcarpathia, and the Old Believers. The last group consists of the remnants of once flourishing isolated communities, mostly in ethnic Russian rural settlements in Bukovina (the so-called *Lypovany*), in Chernihiv, and in the Kherson regions. Numerically and organizationally, it is an insignificant group, without any political relevance. Since the Old Believers, scattered in a few rural communities, are self-centered and do not display missionary zeal, the regime does not treat them any more harshly than it treats religion in general. The Old Believers do not play any supportive or adversary role vis-à-vis the Ukrainian national cause, and only a few individual ethnic Ukrainians share their beliefs.

Reformed Church of Transcarpathia. An organization of ethnic Hungarians, this church is a traditional national denomination of Magyars that historically was an advocate of Hungarian nationalism, mainly in the borderlands. It embraces about half of the Magyars in the area (about 60,000) and maintains about 40 operating churches with about 30 pastors. The pastors are trained in Hungary. Since the Hungarian minority in the Ukrainian SSR belongs to a relatively privileged ethnic group, this church is tolerated, although closely watched; it has not been upbraided for Hungarian nationalism. Given a change in the international context, it could resume its former role as spokesman for Hungarian territorial revisionism.

Evangelical Christians and Baptists. These groups constitute organizationally one body but historically have belonged to various Protestant denominations and sects. When in 1944 the Soviet government decided to legalize Protestant activities, it preferred to deal with one rather than several groups. As a result, Soviet Baptists, along with Pentecostalists and Adventists, formed the All-Union Council of Evangelical Christians and Baptists. In 1966, the council was joined by the Mennonites, ethnic Germans who had had a sizable following among Germans in Ukraine prior to the war. Individual congregations of the two Protestant communities in Western Ukraine, the Reformed (Calvinist) church and another Church of the Augsburg Confession, also joined the council. But the bulk of the faithful of this new church body consisted of Baptists who had acquired a growing following in Eastern Ukraine and who had attempted before, in the 1920s, to create an all-Ukrainian organization of their own.

Presently, the community has its central authority in Moscow, supervising between 1 and 1.5 million believers, half of them in Ukraine. There is a chief presbyter in Kiev for the Ukrainian republic and a district presbyter in each *oblast* (province). Over 80 percent of the communicants in Ukraine are ethnic Ukrainians. For a long time, the Evangelical Baptist community was, in terms of national identification, indifferent. The congregations, mostly in the Eastern

Ukraine, followed the pattern of the Russian Orthodox church—that means that they were Russianized and used mostly Russian as the language of religious functions. In the Western Ukraine, primarily in Volhynia where there is a strong congregation of Evangelical Christians, the language used in church is Ukrainian. However, no Ukrainian-language publications are being used, and only recently has the Ukrainian character of these communities become more pronounced. A hymnal was published in Ukrainian by an underground printing shop, *Kyristianin*. More frequently than before, prayers and sermons are conducted in the Ukrainian language. It appears that the tendency to revive cultural ethnicity is connected with the internal ferment within the Christian-Baptist community. The emergence of a more radical group, known as *Initsiativnyky* (action group), was connected to the awakening of national consciousness among some activists and rank-and-file believers. Yet the *Initsiativnyky* as a whole do not identify themselves with the Ukrainian cause and avoid involvement in political and cultural nationalism. At the same time, they are not instruments of Russian nationalism, as the Russian Orthodox church in many ways tends to be.[11]

Excessively Restricted Religious Groups

A denomination that can be classified as tolerated, but excessively restricted, is the Roman Catholic church, which has not yet been suppressed in Ukraine. It exists on the parish level without any central authority in the republic. All former dioceses on the Ukrainian territory are vacant, the archdiocese of Lviv being only the latest vacancy. There are now only three historical-ethnic and jurisdictional Roman Catholic groups in the Ukrainian SSR.

Catholics in Western Ukraine. The remnants of the Polish Roman Catholics living in the dioceses of Lviv, Lutsk, and parts of Peremyshl-Przemysl, comprise a dozen or so congregations with a score of priests. Here Roman Catholicism is strongly identified with Polish national consciousness. Their number does not exceed a hundred thousand potential followers.

Catholics in Kiev and Odessa. A second group includes these right bank Ukraine and east Ukrainian cities with some Polish and German minorities, i.e., the territory where Soviet rule was established in 1920. Here, the once-flourishing Roman Catholic minority dwindled ethnically (i.e., a decline in the numbers of Poles and Germans) and organizationally to a token presence. There may still be as many as 150-200,000 nominal Roman Catholics, i.e., those who are baptized or whose parents were baptized. However, organizationally this community finds itself in a sorry state. Only a few itinerant priests service large areas between Kiev, Odessa, and Kamianets Podilsk. The existing congregations have minimal formal contacts with the better-organized Roman Catholic communities in Lithuania and Latvia, and even less with Poland. Yet it is known that a majority of the priests servicing this community in Ukraine came from Latvia. For the declining Polish nationality in Ukraine, the Roman Catholic church could become a source of ethnic maintenance and revival. Soviet authorities are aware of this, and are inclined to speed the process of assimilation of the Poles and, eventually, achieve obliteration of their national church.[12]

Catholics in Subcarpathia. A small group of Roman Catholics in Subcarpathia consists of ethnic Hungarians, Slovaks, and Germans. Again, this group lacks hierarchical ties with larger communities; some practical working relations exist with the Roman Catholic church in neighboring Hungary and Slovakia. This community is able to operate on a more or less normal basis.

The fate of Roman Catholics in Ukraine in a peculiar way is tied to that of the Ukrainian Eastern-rite Catholics and to the policy of the Holy See vis-à-vis all the Catholics in Ukraine and, ultimately, in the USSR, since they are parts of the same church.

Jews and Muslims. Two non-Ukrainian and non-Christian religious communities in the Ukrainian SSR fall into the excessively restricted group: the Jews and the Muslims. The first group numbers over half a million potential adherents, but only a fraction of these, mostly in the western *oblasts*, are practicing Jews. There are no more than twenty to thirty registered Jewish congregations. Allegedly there is only one active rabbi in Kiev; in other cities the congregations are presided over by cantors or other leaders. However, Judaism is part of the ethnic heritage of even non-practicing Jews and is therefore a vital component of Jewish national identity. With the exodus of most active members of the Jewish population to the West in the 1970s, not only religion but also the cause of ethnic Jewish survival in Ukraine has been weakened.

The Muslim community in Ukraine used to consist of Crimean Tatars who were uprooted after World War II. Today there are individuals who were transferred here from Muslim areas of the USSR. They do not constitute any organizational base or community. Their individual religious expression, if any, is tied with their ethnic-religious homelands: Azerbaijan, Kazakhstan, Uzbekistan, the Tatar area, etc. The Crimean Tatars, forcibly resettled in Central Asia in 1944, have not been permitted to return to Crimea.

Banned Religious Groups

The fourth category of religions consists of those organizations that have been outlawed by Soviet authorities and are therefore actively persecuted. This category includes the two historic churches—the Ukrainian Autocephalous Orthodox church and the Ukrainian Greek-rite (Uniate) Catholic church—and three smaller sects—the Pentecostals, the Adventists, and the Jehovah's Witnesses. Besides these, there are two other religious organizations in Ukraine that operate outside the law. The Truly Orthodox church (*Istinno-Pravoslavnaiia Tserkov*) was set up in opposition to the legalized and submissive Russian Orthodox church. Its followers (among whom few ethnic Ukrainians are to be found) are fanatical zealots mostly withdrawn from public life and sometimes openly defying the system. The other is the *Initsiativnyky*, a branch of Evangelical Christians and Baptists who broke with the docile leadership of the All-Union Council in the 1960s. The *Initsiativnyky* call for a more independent stand vis-à-vis Soviet authorities, criticize the regime's religious policy, and defy all restrictions imposed on church activities. Georghi Vins, pastor of Kiev, became secretary-general of its underground central authority, the Council of Churches of Evangelical Christian Baptists. As mentioned before, the group was strongly supported by Ukrainian congregations; thanks to this group, the Ukrainian national factor has been recognized among an otherwise cosmopolitan Baptist community. The *Initsiativnyky* also maintain contacts with the exile-based All-Ukrainian Fellowship of Evangelical Christians, a group known for its clear national position.

The other outlawed sects—the Pentecostals, the Adventists, and the Jehovah's Witnesses—are quite militant, based mostly in the rural areas, and consist of 95 percent ethnic Ukrainians. They maintain a closely knit organizational network of small congregations with elected preachers, use private homes or secret outdoor gatherings for religious functions, and, therefore, cannot be easily controlled. Their "home churches" refuse to register. The members often defy strict legislation about religious activities and challenge certain civic obligations (e.g., the draft, atheist schooling of children, blood transfusions). Nationally they are indifferent, although part of their literature, reproduced secretly in the USSR, is in Ukrainian. The groups tend to develop their following in certain areas: the Ukrainian Pentecostals in Volhynia, Podilia, Polisia, and Ternopil *oblasts*; the Adventists in the Chernivtsi *oblast*; and the Jehovah's Witnesses in the Transcarpathian and Crimean *oblasts*. These sects also are spread among Ukrainians dispersed in Siberia, the Kuban region, and Central Asia.[13]

The Ukrainian Historic National Churches

The Ukrainian Orthodox and Ukrainian Greek-Catholic churches are referred to as historic and national churches in the common perception of Ukrainians in the free world as well as in the writings of *samvydav*. These are the traditional churches, in contrast to the new Protestant-inspired denominations and sects that appeared in the second half of the nineteenth and in the twentieth century. They are perceived to be specifically Ukrainian in their cultural context; in fact, the membership of these two churches has been exclusively Ukrainian. Ethnic Russians naturally prefer the Orthodox church integrated with Moscow or, in extremis, the Ukrainian Autonomous Orthodox church under the patriarchal jurisdiction. The two historic churches are now outlawed and are considered reactionary, hostile, anti-Soviet, and anti-communist. Although not recognized by the regime, prohibited, and persecuted, they continue to exist under adverse conditions: the Ukrainian Catholic Uniate church retaining a formal underground structure, and the autocephalists retaining an alternative church ideology and a potential following within the folds of the official Orthodox church.[14]

Ukrainian Greek-Catholic Church

The journalistic labels attached to the Uniate church in the USSR such as the "Church of Silence" or the "Catacomb Church" do not convey its true situation. It is neither a silent religious community nor are its "catacombs" entombed in the underground caves as some would have it. The Eastern-rite Catholics in Ukraine have adopted various modes of existence for the sake of survival. Some consider themselves a "church within a church," while others view themselves as constituting a marginal religious community.

The "church within the church" is the prevalent form of existence. The bulk of the Uniates, forcibly converted to Orthodoxy, still consider themselves Eastern-rite Catholics, even though formally under the jurisdiction of the Moscow patriarchate. They have remained in pectore, and often publicly, Catholics. To average believers, their presence in the Russian Orthodox church is made less embarrassing by the fact that their former priests are serving there, as well as their local successors (who frequently refer to themselves as Catholics), and, given the opportunity, they would return to their ancestral church, which was equally Catholic and Eastern (in rite and spirituality). The liturgy, the services, the customs, the language, and the entire spiritual atmosphere has not changed considerably from what it was before. Moreover, the church is trying hard to preserve its ethnic Ukrainian characteristics.

The now outlawed Uniates also embrace the status of "a church within *another* church." Some of them, especially in urban communities where the Latin-rite Catholic churches still operate, attend these churches to satisfy their spiritual needs (confessions, baptisms, even sometimes nuptial rites). The number of such Ukrainian Catholics is not very high for several reasons: Roman Catholic parishes are sparse; the spiritual needs of those who refuse to attend Orthodox churches are, to a great extent, being taken care of by the Ukrainian Catholic nonregistered or "secret" priests; and identification with Roman Catholicism (which in Ukraine is equivalent to Polish nationality) might be viewed as unpatriotic.

One should consider this option not only an accidental component of a complex religio-national situation, but also a possible concept to preserve Catholicism against apostasy. It is noteworthy that Soviet authorities do prefer such a possibility to the separate operation of illegal Ukrainian Catholic communities. Several sources, including the Vatican, have suggested that under certain conditions, the Soviet government might consent to the registration of Ukrainian Roman Catholic communities in Western Ukraine or, eventually, to the Ukrainianization of existing Roman Catholic parishes. The implications of such an option are serious. Still, the concession undoubtedly would be limited to only a few parishes and thus would not cause a general reversal of the post-1946 trend.

Such a solution would be divisive for the Ukrainian Catholics since the majority would decline to embrace this solution. Finally, such a miniscule "splinter" church would not and could not be in a position to claim spiritual and jurisdictional unity with the Ukrainian Catholic church structure abroad.[15]

Much more interesting and also more troublesome for the regime is the phenomenon of the so-called Uniate "marginal community," or the nonofficial church. These groups are not easy to assess numerically, but are present in each major locality and even in some smaller ones. Usually, the followers are organized informally around unregistered priests, itinerant monks or nuns, and activist lay people. The groups maintain contacts and communication among themselves and communicate with distant congregations as well as with their leadership. The spiritual leadership tends to preserve canonical hierarchy that, of course, is not recognized by civil authorities. Secret bishops have their eparchal territories, although they may live as workers or pensioners in a small village. Moreover, the communicants outside the Ukraine, but still in the USSR, keep in touch with their brethren in the homeland.

The number of priests in Ukraine has been estimated at between three and five hundred. There is a continuous addition of new priests ordained by secret bishops. Soviet sources report on "secret seminaries," that are in reality no more than private training courses conducted by qualified priests for willing candidates. The underground church allegedly has many religious vocations. A great deal of pastoral work is done by the nuns. They usually live in small communities and earn their living as factory workers, medical personnel, or workers on collective farms. Their identities are, in most cases, known to the authorities. Because they do exemplary work at their places of employment, they are harassed but usually tolerated. Still, from time to time arrests do occur. The priests are watched, called to police stations, fined, and even arrested for transgressing legislation concerning religious cults.[15]

It seems that there is a tacit understanding on the local level that if religious activities of the recalcitrant Uniates are not provocative, are not widely known, and are conducted semiprivately (e.g., celebration of Holy Mass at a private home), they can be overlooked. Periodic imprisonments, searches, trials, public "unmaskings" of illegal activities serve to compel, or at least encourage, the Uniates to restrict themselves to low-key and subdued religious work.

Along with the moderate underground Uniate church, there are more radical followers to Uniatism. There is a Uniate dissenters' group, called neo-Uniates by Soviet sources, whose fanatical spokesmen disagree with the established and hierarchical Uniate church. They question the apparent readiness of the Uniate clergy and laity to accommodate the system if it will grant them recognition. They totally reject the Soviet system, refuse to cooperate with it, and call for disobedience.[16]

This radical religious movement started in the obscure Carpathian village of Serednia (in the Ivano-Frankivsk *oblast*) where in 1954, allegedly, the Mother of God appeared to a local woman. The "miracle of Serednia" soon attracted many pilgrims to the site, on some occasions as many as several thousand worshippers. It is known that at least three illegal Ukrainian Catholic priests actively promoted this religious movement. Soviet media and antireligious propaganda initially referred to this group as the *Ihnativtsi* sect, derived from the name of its first leader, Fr. Ihnatii Soltys, who was later imprisoned and sentenced. He was succeeded by another itinerant Uniate priest, Fr. Antin Potochniak. The group's adherents prefer to call themselves *Pokutnyky* (the Penitents), because they preach that the Ukrainian people must repent their sins of the past in order to be delivered from their present yoke.[17]

The established underground Ukrainian Catholic church questioned the veracity of the miracle, and reacted even more critically to certain postulates and practices of the group, such as preaching the end of the world (announced for 1962), prescribing a nine-day penitence and a pilgrimage to the "Holy Place of the Virgin's apparition" in order to be saved, anathematizing Rome for its cooperation with "Antichrist," and proclaiming the "Holy Mountain" in Serednia as a "New Rome" along with the announcement that a "true Pope" had appeared in Ukraine in the person of Arkyierei Emanuil as a "visible Peter II on earth."[18] This led to an actual break between the regular Ukrainian Catholics and the *Pokutnyky* sect. The latter maintained some of its following among the fanatical and desperate opponents of both the regime and Russian Orthodoxy, mostly among the peasants, and most particularly among peasant women. The influence of the *Pokutnyky* weakened in the late 1970s, however.[19]

Soviet sources admit the challenging nature of the *Pokutnyky* movement, particularly its nationalistic-messianic undercurrent. This aspect was especially singled out by a Soviet author, who asserted that the *Pokutnyky*

> are playing on national feelings by asserting that Ukraine, which has been oppressed in captivity and serfdom for long centuries, is being now resurrected by God. Thus, they try to foment hatred of other peoples, primarily of the Russian nation which, allegedly, introduced atheism in Ukraine. Although the *Pokutnyky* are not widely spread, this nonetheless means that under particular conditions there is a possibility of close interaction between religion and nationalism.[20]

The unofficial or marginal church has been surrounded by an aura of martyrdom that might, for certain individuals, become an additional stimulus to be a part of the repressed group or at least to sympathize with the underdog. The existence of the "second" church is verified not only by political and antireligious sources, but also by Orthodox religious figures and publications. In an article, "The Truth about the Union," Bishop Ioan of Zhytomyr and Ovruch wrote:

> Even now a certain number of people in Halychyna stay under the Uniate influence, considering that the Union forcefully imposed on their ancestors, and not the Orthodoxy shared by our forefathers, is the true religion. These people look at Orthodoxy as on a foreign and false faith, lacking grace. This is

a grave mistake. This causes us great sorrow. It is difficult to explain why certain priests and laity in Halychyna, while keeping in mind the servility of the Uniate leadership toward the enemies of the Ukrainian people, are still unable to free themselves from the Uniate yoke. . . . Those believers in Halychyna who are still in the Uniate captivity . . . should reunite with their Mother Orthodox Church, and she will embrace them with love as her faithful sons. [21]

Many secular sources bring home the reality that the Uniate church is alive, its followers even taking initiatives to change their illegal status. A Soviet student of religion, M. Mchedlov, admits that in the Soviet Union there is

a certain revival and activization of former Uniates. They spread rumors among the populace, particularly among those who were converted to the Orthodox Church. They often slander Soviet reality, inspire all kinds of letters to be sent to Soviet authorities demanding the registration of Uniate congregations. They urge the restoration in Ukraine of the Greek Catholic Church, etc. [22]

Mchedlov was commenting on the efforts of the church in the 1960s, but these efforts have continued throughout the 1970s. The movement of petitions and calls for legalization of the outlawed Uniate religious community has become even more insistent, as has been amply documented in religious and national *samvydav* literature of the period.

Equally revealing is the concern of Soviet policy makers in Ukraine, as illustrated by the same author. Mchedlov charges the "Uniate churchmen" with promoting nationalist ideals. He condemns this activity as being "diversionist," anti-Soviet, and antisocialist in nature. "It is not accidental that artificial attempts to revive the Greek Catholic Church in Ukraine, to establish it as an organization, and to unite all existing Ukrainian church entities, have found support equally among the counter-revolutionary emigre clergy and among the secular bourgeois nationalists." [23]

The campaign of defamation of the Uniates conducted by atheists and party agents, echoed also in the writings of the official representatives of the Russian Orthodox church, focuses on the national-political role of the Ukrainian Catholic church, now and in the past. It is not the purpose of this chapter to present a full account of the anti-Uniate campaign in Western Ukraine or to analyze its themes and arguments. Suffice it to say that there is a large number of publications devoted to the problem; it is also a major topic of lectures, seminars, broadcasts, films, and exhibits in the museums of religion and atheism. An author specializing in the anti-Uniate struggle summarized the tasks of vigorous Soviet propaganda against the "remnants" of the Uniates in this manner:

In this connection it is indispensable to expose continually and pointedly the shameful history and pernicious role of the Greek Catholic Church in the social life of our people. It is necessary to disclose the anti-communist substance of the alliance between its leaders and Ukrainian bourgeois nationalism, to prove the futility of attempts by Western reactionary-bourgeois-clerical quarters to revive artificially Uniatism and to exploit religio-nationalist survivals in the struggle against the USSR, the forces of peace and of social progress.[24]

The leaders of the Ukrainian Catholic church have been charged with collaboration with the Germans during World War II. Even the figure of Metropolitan Sheptytsky, who is well known for his clear stand against the Nazi holocaust and who personally contributed to saving the lives of many Jews, has not been spared.[25] The attack has been particularly strong on the present aged spiritual leader of the Ukrainian Catholics, Josyf Cardinal Slipyj in Rome, who himself spent eighteen years in Soviet prisons and labor camps.

Soviet propaganda attacks the efforts of Ukrainian Catholics to organize their church as a particular structure with autonomy and restored traditional institutions, including a patriarchate. That, of course, is anathema to the Kremlin. Agitprop condemns the cause of beatification of Metropolitan Sheptytsky and accuses Cardinal Slipyj of not keeping his promise to stay away from anti-Soviet activity (allegedly made when Khrushchev agreed to release him in 1963). The present pope also is attacked indirectly for his "generous" treatment of Ukrainians in exile: granting them synodal rule, appointing an archbishop-coadjutor to Slipyj with the right of succession to the see of Lviv-Halych (where the union with Rome was declared dissolved three and a half decades ago), or sending special messages to the Ukrainian Catholic hierarchy on the eve of the millennium of Christianity in Ukraine. Radio Vatican Ukrainian-language programs beamed to Ukraine are labeled "nationalist" and accused of sowing national hatred.[26]

In this regard, the church hierarchy of the Russian Orthodox church also takes issue with the Vatican. On two recent occasions there was a strong intervention of Russian hierarchs with the Holy See. One protest was in response to the pastoral letter of Pope John Paul II on the millennium of Ukraine's Christianity; the second protest came in response to the decision of the Ukrainian bishops' synod to solemnly reject the so-called *Sobor* of Lviv, that had declared the Uniate church dissolved.[27]

Ukrainian Autocephalous Orthodox Church

When it comes to the Ukrainian Orthodox church, it is not so much its present situation that arrests attention as the role of the Autocephalists in the past. A Soviet author, writing in the atheist journal, *Liudyna i svit*, described Ukrainian Autocephalist ideology as "a synthesis of clericalism and Ukrainian bourgeois nationalism." The same author specifically singled out the use of the Ukrainian language in liturgical services as an element of nationalism.[28]

Bishops of the "second" autocephaly (1942–44) are attacked, especially the outspoken Metropolitan Mstyslav Skrypnyk, who now heads the most representative branch of the Ukrainian Orthodox church in exile. The continuity of the autocephaly as an alternative concept to the present Russianized Orthodox church is obviously troublesome. Although presently not threatening, it is potentially an alternative to the Russian Orthodox church and might become as attractive as it was in the 1920s or the early 1940s. Therefore, those who shape national and religious policies in Ukraine would prefer to see the Ukrainian Orthodox congregations in exile absorbed by other national Orthodox organizations, including the newly established Orthodox Church of America. Incidentally, the technically non-national Orthodox Church of America is in reality still very Russian and is strongly opposed by Ukrainians in the United States and Canada.[29]

Any work of religious self-promotion on the part of autocephalists in Ukraine is rebuffed by the Soviets, as are the contacts of Ukrainian Orthodox quarters in exile with the ecumenical patriarchate and other churches. The elaborate structure of the official Russian Orthodox church abroad, with many exarchates and missions in the western world, is designed equally to counteract exiled Russian Orthodox church organizations (*zarubezhnaia*) and Ukrainian ones.

Soviet Response

Both national churches are thorns in the side of the regime: the existing Russian Orthodox church is tolerated as the lesser "evil," while the Orthodox Church in Ukraine is granted some insignificant concessions (e.g., displaying its Ukrainian features) in order to neutralize "nationalist" propaganda emanating from the Uniates and Autocephalists.

The Philosophy Institute of the Academy of Science of the Ukrainian SSR, among others, was instructed by the authorities to expose the allegedly harmful relationship between Ukrainian churches and bourgeois nationalism. Professor O. Yevdokimenko from Kiev Academy spoke in May 1970 in Ivano-Frankivsk, at a republic scholarly conference devoted to the subject. According to the journal, *Filosofs'ka dumka*, he analyzed conceptual and organizational ties among the Uniate, Catholic, and Orthodox clerical circles and the bourgeois nationalists. Yevdokimenko stated that along with other weapons in its ideological arsenal, bourgeois nationalism is using religion as well. Being likewise conservative and "reactionary" systems, both religion and bourgeois nationalism indulge in a common struggle against progressive forces. They can be opposed only from the position of Marxist-Leninist scientific communism, including atheism, and, most important, by propagating the principles of proletarian internationalism and the friendship of peoples.[30]

A Soviet atheist publication repudiated the proposition advanced by advocates of religious freedom that the Ukrainian people are religious by nature, that the Ukrainian psyche is inherently a religious one.[31] The religiosity to which the Ivano-Frankivsk conference participants and some other Soviet authors refer, however, does exist in the Soviet "classless" society, although its supposed foundation in class exploitation should have been terminated some time ago. If it is true that religion and nationalism are active and mutually supportive, then other motivations might affect the religio-nationalist coalescence as a unity.

Soviet writers have outlined some of the motivations of those still religiously active in Ukraine. First—according to these writers—there are forces (primarily from outside Soviet society) that use religion in an attempt to disseminate among Soviet people bourgeois ideas and ways of life. Second, the same agents, along with some internal foes of the Soviet regime, intend to use religion to revive the remnants of bourgeois nationalism. To this end, according to Soviet spokesmen, some churchmen pretend that religion preserves national tradition. It is, according to V. Tancher, presented as the champion for the conservation of national traditions. The religiosity of a people is further portrayed as the virtue of national selfhood, while the performance of religious rituals and the observance of holidays are valued as expressions of a national character.[32]

The same author specifically singled out Ukrainian Catholics to criticize their nationalist attitude, in particular their attempts to foster opposition between Ukrainians and Russians. As long ago as 1968, Tancher wrote that

> all churches serve the interests of the exploiting classes. But the Uniate Church played a particular reactionary role. Uniate believers desired opposition between the Ukrainian and Russian nations. They wanted to see these countries quarrel; they attempted to isolate these two friends from each other. Religious differences shook the foundations of Ukraine's national unity.[33]

Religion and nationalism are serious obstacles and ideological foes to two programmatic values of Soviet communism, internationalism and atheism. They are presented as reactionary prejudice, still alive in Soviet society, trying to counter Marxist-Leninist ideas. Because of their "reactionary" nature and the survival of past traditions, they interact and support each other. "Religiosity motivates national isolationism, and nationalist vestiges frequently stimulate religious prejudices," according to another Soviet author.[34]

This is relevant, in particular, in the Ukrainian case, where two "traditional" churches oppose the Russian character of the communist regime and its Russificatory nationalities policy. The idea has been spelled out by an author specializing in antireligious and antinationalist pamphlets. "The Ukrainian bourgeois nationalist ideologists," he writes,

> assert that religion (in its Uniate and autocephalous variants) constitutes, so to say, the "spiritual support" of the Ukrainian nation and impedes its assimilation into the Soviet multinational state. From this erroneous assumption, they arrive at the conclusion about the anti-national character of atheism which supposedly aims at the denationalization and Russification of the people within the USSR.[35]

That observation is apropos. Not only representatives of church organizations, but also secular critics of Soviet religious policy, point to the fact that the Soviet ideological struggle in Ukraine is aimed simultaneously at both religion and nationalism.

Dissidents' Voices

In its first issue (January 1970), *Ukrainsky Visnyk* (the *Ukrainian Herald*) published a detailed, documented survey of the reprisals against Ukrainian Catholics in the late 1960s. It mentioned two dozen Uniate priests who were arrested, tried, or harassed in other ways for their priestly activity.[36] The same issue featured a lengthy statement by a persecuted Ukrainian Catholic priest, Hryhorii Budzynsky, in which the author questioned charges raised against him that led to his sentencing in 1945 and resentencing in 1947. In the same article, Fr. Budzynsky criticized the Soviet government and the Russian Orthodox church for their roles in the forcible dissolution of the Ukrainian Catholic church in 1946. It was the atheist government and its police agents (of the NKVD) that convened the Lviv Synod with a view to the formal suppression of the union with Rome, argued Budzynsky. He also indicted the Russian Orthodox church for its regrettable service to the secular regime, simultaneously spelling out his nationalist sentiments:

In the past, the Russian Church truthfully and faithfully served the robber imperialism of the Russian czars and in the long course of its history, has specialized in criminal acts. Its leadership severely persecuted the best sons and daughters of the Ukrainian nation; it hated the Ukrainian language and fanatically fought against it.[37]

A short note in the journal's second issue illustrated how religion and national culture are intertwined in everyday relations. In *Visnyk's* account,

fines of 30 rubles were imposed on some 30 villagers of Kosmach by the decision of the Kosiv *raion* executive committee of Ivano-Frankivsk *oblast* for having gone carolling on Christmas. About a hundred persons were interrogated in this connection. As a result, the priest of the Kosmach church, Vasyl Romaniuk, was prevented from performing his priestly functions for a month. Such was the decision of the plenipotentiary for religious affairs in Ivano-Frankivsk *oblast*. The reason for the charge was that Father Romaniuk had been telling people, in his sermons, to dress in their Hutsul folk garb, not to sell antique objects to tourists, and, in general, to preserve Hutsul traditions. When asked what is wrong with that, the plenipotentiary replied: "*Eto pakhnet natsionalizmom!*" [This smells like nationalism.][38]

It was Valentyn Moroz who, among national dissenters, most strikingly demonstrated the close ties between the traditional Ukrainian church and the nationalist idea in his essay, "Chronicle of Resistance."[39] Religion and religiosity, in

Moroz's view, are chiefly expressed through the national spirit and national culture. Although disseminated only as *samvydav* writing and published only in the West, the essay made a strong impression on the dissident movement in Ukraine. This is in part why official Soviet propaganda addresses some of Moroz's ideas.

Moroz, a historian and writer, views the role of the church in Ukrainian society as an essential component of national life. "The Church entered so deeply into the civilization and spirituality of the Ukrainian people that it is inconceivable to get at it without destroying the entire spiritual structure of the nation," he declared, and urged his contemporaries to resist any encroachment against religion and the beliefs of the people.[40]

In addition to Budzynsky and Moroz—the former a Uniate priest, the latter an Orthodox layman—other prominent religious dissenters of the 1970s include Orthodox priest Vasyl Romaniuk, Orthodox layman Lev Lukianenko, and two Catholic laymen, Josyf Terela and Vasyl Barladian.

Romaniuk, a baptized Uniate from Western Ukraine who embraced Orthodoxy, experienced difficulties early on with the regime and the church hierarchy. Before his imprisonment, and even more after, he voiced his opposition to the regime's repressive policies. He sent many petitions to the pope, the World Council of Churches, the Ukrainian hierarchy abroad, and others, calling for intercession on behalf of religious freedom in Soviet Ukraine.[41]

Lukianenko, a lawyer from Eastern Ukraine who had spent fifteen years in prison for nationalist activities, joined the Kiev Helsinki monitoring group in 1977. In 1978 he was arrested again and sentenced for a second time. Among his known writings there are two pieces on religious subjects. The first, "A Christmas Message to the Stubborn Atheists," presented Lukianenko's severe criticism of atheism and Marxism. The second, a letter to Metropolitan Filaret, urged the defense of religion against regime discrimination. The author challenged the submissive prelate to intervene in the debate over the constitutional draft to ensure that the legal rights of all religions would be incorporated in it, and that the right of atheistic propaganda would be counterbalanced by a right of religious propaganda. Incidentally, both dissenters made their *profession de foi* as adherents of Ukrainian autocephaly.[42]

Terela's and Barladian's many letters and petitions reflect the fate of persecuted Catholics of the Eastern rite in the USSR. In a lengthy letter to Yuri Andropov that reads like an indictment of the system itself, Terela wrote: "I am a Christian—more specifically, a Ukrainian Catholic, to whom it is prohibited, under the threat of imprisonment, to take part in religious functions, that is, to confess, to christen children, to repent, and to celebrate religious holidays without being labeled a 'militant Catholic.' The Ukrainian Catholic Church is in the catacombs."[43]

Religious themes have entered into *samvydav* literary works of the 1970s. Mykola Rudenko and Oles Berdnyk, two writers and poets active in the Kiev monitoring group, have enriched the religious samizdat by their philosophical-mystical writings promoting theistic and libertarian thought. Other poets, like Ihor Kalynets, Vasyl Stus, and others, are motivated by religious symbolism.[44] In the unofficial visual arts being created in Ukraine today, Christian motifs serve as an inspiration to many artists.

Along the same lines, religious values have been assessed by a literary critic, Yevhen Sverstiuk, in his inspiring essay, *The Cathedral in Scaffolding*. In the author's view, religion, spirituality, and culture constitute primordial values that constantly enrich humanity and give real and genuine dimensions to existence. "How many sacrifices our people made in order to pass to posterity the true human ideals, beliefs, selfless love of truth and devotion to God of our forefathers!" exclaimed Sverstiuk.[45]

Throughout the many works of literature and art of the new Ukrainian generation, a close relationship between religion and nationality is reflected as a *signum temporis*, a writing on the wall amid the gloomy reality of our times.

Conclusion

The religious-national panorama of Ukraine, analyzed in its past and present dimensions, provides us with several models of underlying spiritual-ideological values, the type of organization based on them, and, finally, certain political concepts resulting therefrom.

In the first model, the Ukrainian national churches, viz., the Ukrainian Greek-Catholic (or Uniate) and the Ukrainian Autocephalous Orthodox, represent a single pattern: religiosity is treated as the "national character" of Ukrainians; and a separate, indigenous Ukrainian cultural development, as opposed to the Russian one, is stressed. Here national culture has been inspired by religion for over one thousand years and therefore a symbiosis of religion and nationality is taken for granted. Religion also has affected the revival of national consciousness in modern times and the awakened nationalism contributes to the articulation of national church ideology. This then becomes a challenge to broader universal ecclesiastical communities (Roman Catholic or Orthodox). Religion, in principle, tends to identify with ethnic nationalism, in this model. Politically the first model expresses itself in the quest for national statehood.

The proponents of Russian Orthodoxy, in the next model, also assume the religious nature of Eastern Slavs as a starting point and see an essential cultural factor in the millennium-long common Russian past of Eastern Christianity. Kiev Rus', as the cradle of all-Russian religious-cultural heritage (and, even more so, Muscovite Russia), molded its own unique expression of Orthodox spirituality that was simultaneously Russian-national and supranational (in a regional Slavic context). From this there developed a Russian national church with Slavophile and sometimes universalist overtones. The Russian Orthodox church was, in many ways, the Eastern counterpart of the Roman Catholic church. The difference is that the Roman Catholic church became international over time, claiming the fidelity of numerous European sovereigns. Russian Orthodoxy, on the other hand, closely identified itself with one sovereign, the czar of Russia. The Russian church became nationalist—not in a narrow ethnic sense, but in a pan-Russian and pan-Slavic sense, integrating many ethnic elements in the process of their gradual Russification.

Other Christian religions in today's Ukraine hardly parallel either of these patterns. Their motivating values are purely religious ones and are not rooted in the ethnosocial past of the nation. When the Ukrainian national movement and consciousness appeared as a reaction to the dominating nationalisms of neighboring countries, all Protestant groups and denominations maintained neutrality. Some of them may have been responsive, for practical reasons, to the use of the Ukrainian language, but their motivation in this regard was not to strengthen Ukrainian ethnic consciousness and national aspirations, but simply to establish as broad a presence as possible in the Ukrainian community. Moreover, these sectarian groups were in their very nature international and addressed themselves equally to all ethnic groups. The result is non-national religious organizations. Their civic attitude is loyalty to any system willing to tolerate religious pluralism. Cosmopolitanism is their preferred concept insofar as international relations are concerned. It is understandable, then, why rigid Ukrainian, Russian, or Polish nationalists would view Protestantism with much suspicion as an alien body.

Finally, the fourth model, Soviet secular antireligion, possessing some quasi-religious features and functions, fits our analysis this way. Its underlying values are scientific atheism and the claim of internationalism (so-called proletarian internationalism). Yet, within the definite historical context, the Soviet model replaced initial Marxist rootless internationalism with Russian culture, the historical and geopolitical heritage of imperial Russia, as a more tangible mobilizational value to shape a new man and society.

These values materialize in the notion of the Soviet people as a new sociocultural and psychological entity, consisting of many ethno-national elements. The formation of a "Soviet people" (*Sovietskii narod*) is now an expressed goal of Soviet social engineering. Since it is, at least under present conditions, inconceivable that such an entity would be a nationless hybrid, the Soviet people is being shaped around the Russian national culture and language. From a religious standpoint, the pretension is to be the ideal form of the City of Man on earth. (See table 4.1.)

As much as the two Ukrainian national churches coalesce in one model, the two others, the Orthodox-Russian and the secular communist, also tend to converge, partly for practical and partly for more serious ideological reasons. The case of present Soviet nationalities and religious policies largely proves it. As a result, a protracted tension between the two ensues, with the intermediary model being temporarily neutral.

Table 4.1. The city of man on earth

Underlying values	Institutional-sociological concept	International concept	Political concept
Model 1			
Religious psychology	National or particular church	Ethnic Ukrainian membership exclusively	Nationalism
Culture rooted in Christian traditions	Church autonomy /autocephaly		Independent national state
National consciousness			Democracy
Model 2			
Russian religious heritage	Orthodox pan-Russian church with ecumenic aspirations	Religion of all East Slavic (Russian) peoples	Soviet-Russian nationalism
Common Russian ethno-cultural unity		Open to non-Slavs	Unity of historical Russia
Traditionalism /messianism			Autocracy
Model 3			
Pure religious consciousness	International church organization	Open to all	Loyalty to any regime respecting rights
Anti-establishment subculture		International cooperation, brotherhood	Cosmopolitan
National neutralism and pluralism			Democracy
Model 4			
Scientific atheism	"Soviet people"	Rapprochement and mutual cultural enrichment	Soviet commonwealth
Internationalism	"New Soviet man and society"	Merger of nations	Continuity of Russian Empire
Primacy of Russian culture		Friendship	Totalitarianism

Religion and Nationalism in Ukraine

1. The antiquated terms *Ruthenia, Ruthenian* (Rus', Rus'kyi) have been synonomous with the modern terms *Ukraine, Ukrainian*, and preceded the latter.

2. A comprehensive treatment of church history in Ukraine in relation to East European developments can be found in A.M. Amann, *Abriss der ostslawischen Kirchen* (Vienna: Verlag Herder, 1950).

3. The founder and ideologist of Ukrainian autocephaly, Metropolitan V. Lypkivskyi, emphatically stressed national particularities of religion in Ukraine. He stated that "the popular enthusiasm for the Ukrainian Church derives from a typical national feature: the people started to like their own church for its national particularism. This means that even now the people continue to view their Church through the eyes of their seventeenth century ancestors who considered the Ukrainian Church as their national attribute." See *Istoriia Ukrainskoi Tserkvy* (Winnipeg: Trident Press, 1961), p. 55.

4. Close ties between Ukrainian autocephaly and the nascent national revival were demonstrated by B. R. Bociurkiw in "Soviet Church Policy in the Ukraine, 1919-1939" (unpublished diss., University of Chicago, 1961), as well as in his recent article "Ukrainianization Movements within the Russian Orthodox Church and the Autocephalous Orthodox Church," *Harvard Ukrainian Studies* 3-4 (1979-80), 1:92-111.

5. V. Markus, "The Suppressed Church: Ukrainian Catholics in the Soviet Union," in *Marxism and Religion in Eastern Europe*, ed. R. T. de George and J. P. Scanlan (Dordrecht, Holland and Boston: D. Reidel, 1976) pp. 119-20.

6. The label comes from the name of national leader Symon Petlura, who led the struggle for independence in 1918-20 in Ukraine and with whose name the aspirations for an autocephalous church are connected.

7. Fifteen eparchies have administrating bishops and three eparchial sees are vacant (i.e., other bishops are in charge of their administration). The present status of the Orthodox hierarchy in Ukraine is compiled on the basis of the monthly journal *Pravoslavnyi Visnyk* (Kiev, 1976-78), and *Pravoslavnyi Tserkovnyi Kalendar 1979* (Moscow, 1979).

8. Archbishop of Lviv Makarii Oksiuk issued in 1950 a pastoral letter to the West Ukrainian eparchies reminding the former Uniate priests of "sixteen points" to be corrected in church rituals and liturgical use. See V. Markus, "Religion and Nationality: The Uniates of Ukraine," in *Religion and Atheism in the USSR and Eastern Europe*, ed. B. Bociurkiw and J. Strong (London: Macmillan, 1975), p. 107.

9. *Ukrainsky Visnyk 7-8, 1974* (Paris/Baltimore/London: Smoloskyp, 1975), p. 143.

10. An optimistic official view of the Russian Orthodox church in Ukraine is presented by Archbishop Makarii in *Pravoslavia na Ukraini* (Kiev: Ukraina Society, 1980). The pamphlet also has appeared in English under the title *Orthodox Church in Ukraine* (Kiev, 1980). The author is a member of the board of the *Ukraina* Society, which cultivates cultural ties with foreign countries.

11. Scattered information on the present situation of Evangelical Baptists and other Protestant denominations in Ukraine can be found in the bimonthly journal *Pislanets Pravdy* (Chicago), in *Liudyna i svit* (Kiev), and in other samizdat sources. See also *Religious Minorities in the Soviet Union*, Report no. 1 (London: Minority Rights Groups, 1973).

12. Valuable facts on Roman Catholics in Ukraine were reported by J. Mirski, "O sytuacji Katolikòw w ZSSR" in *Kultura*(Paris), no. 6 (1977), pp. 26-44. This author covered the subject in the article "The Religious Situation of Ukrainians in Poland and of Poles in Ukraine" in *Poland and Ukraine: Past and Present*, ed. P. Potichnyj (Edmonton/Toronto: Canadian Institute of Ukrainian Studies, 1980). The article has been republished in the Polish samizdat journal *Oboz* (Warsaw), no. 1 (September 1981).

13. This author presented a survey of religious groups in present-day Ukraine in a paper entitled *Current Religious Movements in the Soviet Ukraine*, delivered May 25, 1979, at the annual conference of the Canadian Association of Slavists, Saskatchewan, Sask.

14. Today there is no formal or even underground organization of the Ukrainian Orthodox Autocephalous church in the USSR; its sympathizers are in the official Russian Orthodox church trying to Ukrainianize it although they voice a preference for a national church. Dissenters like Rev. Vasyl Romaniuk and lawyer Lev Lukianenko have expressed their adherence to the concept of autocephaly. Their writings are compiled by this author in *Viruiucha Ukraina (The Faith in Ukraine)* (Rome: Ukrainian Catholic University, 1983). See also V. Romaniuk, *A Voice in the Wilderness*, trans. and ed. J. Dobczansky (Wheaton, Ill.: Center for Study of Religion under Communism, 1980), p. 126.

15. The sad situation of Ukrainian Catholics is described in a collective letter (signed by the "faithful of the Ukrainian Church in the USSR") to Pope John Paul II, first published in the Polish *samizdat Spotkania*, no. 16 (1981) and then in *Glaube in der 2. Welt* 10, no. 4 (1982), pp. 127-30. It also has been covered in a moving report, with pictures, by Cardinal Josyf Slipyj, exiled head of that church, in an article, "The Church of the Martyrs," *The Mirror* (Königstein), no. 2, (1981).

16. V. Bodnar, "Osobennosti razvitiia ateizma v kulturnoi revoliutsii v natsionalnoi respublike (na materialakh zapadnykh oblastei Ukrainskoi SSR)," " *Ateizm i sotsialisticheskaia kultura* (Moscow, 1971), pp. 51-52.

17. Markus, "Religion and Nationality," p. 111.

18. *Pokutnyky* are briefly but comprehensively presented by B. Bociurkiw, "Religion and Nationalism in Contemporary Ukraine," in *Nationalism in the USSR and Eastern Europe in the Era of Brezhnev and Kosygin*, ed. G. W. Simmonds (Detroit: University of Detroit Press, 1977), pp. 86-87. Information on "Arkhyierei Emanuil" is found in the pokutnyky document "Letter from Heaven," to which Bociurkiw makes reference.

19. See recent Soviet attacks against Pokutnyky in a pamphlet by A. Shysh, *Uniaty-Pokutnyky:Khto vony?* (Uzhhorod, 1978), p. 135; and *Liudyna i Svit*, no. 4 (1978).

20. Bodnar, "Osobennosti," p. 52.

21. *Pravoslavnyi Visnyk* (Kiev), no. 12 (1980), pp. 26-27.

22. M. Mchedlov, *Katolitsizm* (Moscow, 1970), pp. 242-43.

23. Ibid., p. 245.

24. I. Myhovych, *Uniatska Tserkva i ukrainskyi burzhuaznyi natsionalizm* (Kiev, 1981), p. 141.

25. In 1981, a film was produced titled *The Secret of the Saint George Cathedral* for showing in Western Ukraine. It was a strong attack against the late Metropolitan Sheptytsky.

26. A. Biskup, "Uniatski radiodyversanty," *Liudyna i Svit*, no. 12 (1980), p. 59.

27. The letters exchanged between the patriarch of Moscow and the Holy See concerning the latter issue are found in *Informatsionnyi Biuleten*, no. 2 (Moscow patriarchate, Department of External Relations), April 8, 1981.

28. *Liudyna i svit*, no. 9 (1980), pp. 60-61.

29. See Ukrainian Orthodox periodicals published in exile: *Ukrainske pravoslavne slovo* (South Bound Brook, N.J.) and *Visnyk* (Winnipeg, Canada).

30. *Filosofska dumka* (Kiev), no. 6 (1970), p. 103.

31. V. Moskalets, "Sprostovano zhyttiam, pro tak zvannu relihiinist' psykholohii ukraintsiv," *Liudyna i svit*, no. 2 (1982), pp. 34-36.

32. V. Tancher, "Ateizm i ateistychne vykhovannya," *Filosofska dumka*, no. 2 (1974), p. 53; see also Tancher, *Religioznyie perezhitki i ikh preodoleniia* (Kiev, 1979).

33. *Pravda Ukrainy* (Kiev), no. 28 (1968).

34. V. Mykhailov, "Internatsionalne i ateistychne vykhovannia u trudovykh kolektyvakh," *Liudyna i svit*, no. 4 (1978), p. 7.

35. I. Myhovych, "Rozvinchuiuchy ideolohiiu uniatstva," *Liudyna i svit*, no. 10 (1981), p. 56.

36. *Ukrainsky Visnyk 1-2, 1970* (Paris/ Baltimore: Smoloskyp, 1971), pp. 56-63.

37. Ibid., p. 71.

38. Ibid., p. 205.

39. English editions of Moroz's works: *Chronicle of Resistance in Ukraine* (Baltimore: Smoloskyp, 1970); *Report from the Beria Reserve* (Chicago: Cataract Press, 1974); *Boomerang: The Works of Valentyn Moroz* (Baltimore: Smoloskyp, 1974). French edition: *Chronique de la résistance* (Paris: Edition PIUF, 1977).

40. *Chronique de la résistance*, p. 131, trans. V. Markus.

41. See Romaniuk, *Voice in the Wilderness*, pp. 19-69.

42. *Zupynit Kryvosuddia. Sprava Levka Lukianenka*, ed. S. Sadovsky (New York: Suchasnist, 1980), pp. 86-91; Letter to Metropolitan Filaret in *Syoboda* (Jersey City, N.J., Oct. 27, 1978).

43. J. Terela, *Notes from a Madhouse* (Baltimore/Washington/Toronto: Smoloskyp, 1977), p. 1; quoted here and translated by author from *Suchasnist* (Munich), nos. 7-8 (1977), p. 217.

44. Some *samvydav* literary works of Ukrainian poets and writers recently were published abroad: I. Kalynets, *Poezii z Ukrainy* (Brussels: Lettres et Art, 1970) and *Pidsumovuiuchy movchannia* (Munich: Suchasnist, 1971); M. Rudenko, *Khrest* (Baltimore: Smoloskyp, 1977) and *Prozrinnia* (Baltimore/ Toronto: Smoloskyp, 1978); O. Berdnyk, *Blakytnyi Koval* (Baltimore: Smoloskyp, 1975), *Ukraina Sichi Vichnoi* (Baltimore: Smoloskyp, 1977), *Sviata Ukraina* (Baltimore/Toronto: Smoloskyp, 1980), and *Prometei* (Munich: Ukrainske Vydavnytstvo, 1981).

45. Y. Sverstiuk, *Sobor u Ryshtovanni* (Paris/Baltimore: PIUF and Smoloskyp, 1970), p. 73. Sverstiuk wrote his essay, *The Cathedral in Scaffolding*, to defend O. Honchar and his novel, *The Cathedral* (1969), against unjustified party criticism and to expand his own humanistic and national views on Ukrainian culture. The novel, which exalts Ukrainian past and national traditions, has been published in three editions in the Soviet Ukraine (the fourth was confiscated after publication) and in four editions outside the USSR. Sverstiuk evaluates Honchar's work: "The fundamental meaning of O. Honchar's novel lies in the search for the support point of spirituality and for the sources of humanness, as well as in the exploration of traditions and sacred places to which, in a world of disrupted standards, people cling in order to preserve their being and essence" (p. 29).

II

Religion and Nationality: The Uniates of the Ukraine

Vasyl Markus

The close relationship between organised national religion and nationality is striking in the East European socio-cultural context. Many religious denominations acquired national designations, e.g. Hungarian Church (Calvinists), Polish (Roman Catholic), German (Lutheran), Ruthenian or Ukranian (Uniate, i.e. Catholic Church of Byzantine–Slavonic Rite), etc. In certain cases the religious–ethnic identity has been so prevalent that ethnically different communities of the same religion were considered by common people as also being religiously different.[1]

Eastern Christianity in its two denominational manifestations – Orthodox and Catholic – has become the national religion in the Ukraine, differentiating the native society from past and present dominating nationalities and/or state powers, whether Polish, Russian (at least in the case of the Uniates) or Austro–Hungarian.[2] Practically all serious Ukrainian historians, from conservative Vyacheslav Lypynsky to socialist-populist Mykhaylo Hrushevsky, concur in attributing to the Church the pre-eminent role in the cultural, social and political development of the nation.[3] To a greater extent than elsewhere, religion in the Ukraine has been a nation-building factor. The Ukrainian Cossack political-military organisation in 16th–18th centuries closely identified itself with the Ukrainian Orthodox Church, although the common Orthodox religion which they shared with the Russians was partly instrumental in the political orientation of Cossack leadership towards the 'Orthodox Tsar of All Russia'. Ukrainian Cossacks proudly referred to themselves as the 'defenders of the Orthodox faith'.

When the Church lost its autonomous status and national

character, as in the case of the Orthodox Church in the Russian-ruled Ukraine from the second half of the 18th century, the concept of nationality was emptied of its dynamic content. Before long the Church in the Ukraine, subjected to the centralized rule of St Petersburg, became an instrument of Tsarist autocracy and Russification. The 20th-century movement for church reforms in the Ukraine aimed not only at emancipation from secular rule but also at the Ukrainianisation of the Church, in other words, at its de-Russification. Hence the establishment of the Ukrainian Autocephalous Orthodox Church in 1919–21 which was liquidated by the Soviet regime when its continuous development threatened the designs of Stalin's nationalities policy.[4]

The Uniate Church in the western regions of the Ukraine initially had the possibility of becoming a bridgehead for Polish influence, including cultural Polonisation of the Ukrainian élite. However, due to complex social, political and psychological circumstances, it has fulfilled quite an opposite function.[5] In the Austrian part of the Ukraine, since the end of the 18th century, the Ruthenian (Ukrainian) Church undertook the role of the national catalyst – particularly in the national-cultural revival during the 19th and 20th centuries. Western Ukrainians, termed ironically by Poles as the *naród chłopów i panów* (the people of the priests and peasants), underwent, in the last 150 years, a process of radical transformation into a political nation with strong nationalistic undercurrents, manifested to a great degree through the Ukrainian Catholic (Uniate) Church.

Ruling powers, made apprehensive by the emergence of a Ukrainian political movement, autonomist or separatist, directed their moves against the Ukrainian Church. They recognised that if the native Church with its Ukrainian–Byzantine rite could be taken from the people, or at least weakened in its components, the Ukrainians would become an easy target of Russification, Polonisation, Slovakisation, or eventually, of any type of assimilation in the countries of Ukrainian diaspora. Valentyn Moroz, a young Ukrainian historian, sentenced in 1970 to fourteen years' imprisonment and exile in the U.S.S.R., wrote:

> How often in history has religion saved a nation! Particularly, in the situations when change of religion was equivalent to the change of nationality. In a number of villages of Kholm

region the Ukrainians spoke Polish. But they remained Ukrainians as long as they belonged to the Ukrainian religion and Church. Likewise, a Polish family in a Ukrainian village in Zhytomyr region or in Podillya throughout the centuries remained Polish (without even knowing the Polish language) as long as they were Roman Catholic.[6]

Several interrelated factors, causes and consequences, may be singled out to explain the religion-nationality coalescence in the Ukraine, past and present. Historically, at least during the period of the Ukraine's political self-assertion, there has been little if any conflict between the native Church, society and political power structure. Despite the Byzantine origin of Kievan Christianity, the Kievan State (Rus'–Ukraine) was one of the few medieval states in Europe where the Church–State relationship was quite harmonious, i.e. without the dominance of one power over the other. The Ukrainian-Ruthenian aristocracy was denationalised in the course of the 16th–17th centuries as a result of the loss of political autonomy and subsequent embracement of Roman Catholicism and Polish culture by aristocrats. In the Polish-ruled part of the Ukraine, for a long time, the only spokesmen and representatives of the Ukrainian people were members of the church hierarchy and other leading churchmen ('spiritual princes').

Moreover, the Ukrainian lower clergy fully shared the fate of the people as many of them were at the bottom of the social ladder in the feudal state of Poland–Lithuania. Married clergy with large families, although a distinct social class, continuously remained an organic component of Ukrainian nationality. The sons and daughters of priests constituted in the 19th and 20th centuries the class of populist intelligentsia, the prime movers in national revival. Thus, under the most strenuous conditions of national existence (complete loss of political autonomy), the native religion remained the last refuge of ethnicity, and as such has become the vehicle of national renaissance. It was the spiritual source and institutional framework of cultural, literary and artistic creativity, so indispensable in modern nationalism.

In at least two stages of the East European nation-building process (ethnic awakening, cultural self-assertion, the drive for political self-determination), the rule of religion was primordial and politically indispensable. The almost complete absence of the Orthodox clergy in the initial stages of the national movement in the Eastern Ukraine (under Russia) resulted in its relatively late emergence and in its general weakness until the Revolution of 1917. Similarly, among the Byelorussians, the national awakening during the 19th and 20th centuries was delayed due, among other factors, to the absence of nationally inspired clergy. It seems that the early liquidation (1839) of the Uniate Church in Byelorussia had a negative effect on the development of the Byelorussian national movement.[7]

SOVIET RELIGIOUS POLICY *vis-à-vis* UNIATES
SINCE 1945

In the light of these observations, it is obvious why Soviet policymakers were seriously preoccupied with the problem of religion and nationality in the Ukraine. Their policy resulted in the forceful liquidation of two intrinsically national churches during the first thirty years of Soviet rule in the Ukraine.

The Ukrainian Autocephalus Orthodox Church (U.A.P.T.s), headed by Vasyl Lypkivsky, was destroyed by the Soviet authorities in the 1930s. The Autocephalous Church under Metropolitan Polikarp Sikorsky, revived during the German occupation in 1942–44, was also suppressed after the Soviet recapture of the Ukraine and displaced by the official Russian Orthodox Church.[8]

The Uniate Church in the Western Ukraine[9] presented the Soviet regime with more difficult problems. In 1944–45, when the Soviets incorporated the West Ukrainian *oblasti* into the Ukrainian S.S.R., there existed a well-organised religious community of over four million faithful, an entire hierarchy and a Western-educated, nationalistic clergy numbering almost three and a half thousand. The political authorities, in close co-operation with the Russian Orthodox Church, succeeded within five years in formally liquidating the Uniate Church in Galicia and Trans-Carpathia, as well as in the Ukrainian-populated part of Czechoslovakia. The story of this modern 'conversion' is well known, and need not be related here in detail.[10]

After the death of Metropolitan Andrei Sheptytsky (1864–1944) and the succession to the Metropolitan See of Halych of Archbishop Josyf Slipyj, the latter attempted to accommodate his

Church to the new political reality. In December 1944 Metropolitan Slipyj sent a delegation to Moscow in the hope of getting the Soviet Government to recognise the legal status of the Uniate (Greek Catholic) Church in the U.S.S.R. The Soviet authorities did not commit themselves since the plan for the liquidation of the Uniate Church was evidently already conceived.

Just before World War II ended, all Uniate bishops on Soviet territory were arrested and transferred to a Kiev prison along with two others from Peremyshl (now in Polish territory). Soon after an Action Initiative Group was formed, headed by the priest Havryil Kostelnyk, with the aim of 'reuniting' the Greek Catholics with the Russian Orthodox Church. The Group received immediate recognition from the Government of the Ukrainian S.S.R. as the sole provisional church–administrative body over Uniate parishes.

With the help of Party and secret police officials, the Group collected signatures from priests adhering to its programme. These were extorted either under the threat of arrest or, simply, under the false pretence that they were only a declaration of loyalty to the regime. During 1945 alone, over 800 priests were arrested, temporarily held or deported. In response to the activities of the Action Group, and to the persecution of the Uniates, 300 priests sent a letter of protest to the Government in Moscow requesting freedom of religion for the Greek Catholic Church; a freedom guaranteed to all citizens by the Soviet constitution. Instead of answering this plea, the Government intensified the terror against the 'recalcitrants'. At the same time, Patriarch Alexii of Moscow addressed an appeal to the Uniates 'to break all the ties with the Vatican'.

In this climate of fear, the Action Group, with the help of the Orthodox Church hierarchy and Soviet authorities, prepared the final act of the drama. On 8–10 March 1946 a Synod of the Greek Catholic Church was held in Lviv attended by 214 priests and 19 laymen, plus participants from the Orthodox hierarchy and representatives of the Government. The Synod resolved to break the Union of Brest with Rome (1596) and to 'reunite' with the Russian Orthodox Church. The Patriarch of Moscow and the Soviet Government immediately sanctioned this decision. The Lviv Synod was strongly condemned by many Uniates in the U.S.S.R. and by Ukrainians, as well as Vatican spokesmen in the

West as being an 'uncanonical' political tool of an atheist regime, deserving the name of a 'pseudo-Synod'.[11]

None of the nine Ukrainian Uniate bishops attended the Lviv Synod because just before the Synod they had been secretly tried in Kiev. The members of the Uniate hierarchy were sentenced (for alleged collaboration with Nazi occupation authorities and for 'war crimes') to long years of imprisonment and hard labour. Most of the bishops died in prison or concentration camps.[12]

The Uniate Church in Trans-Carpathia (formerly a part of Czechoslovakia and incorporated into the U.S.S.R. in June 1945) was 'reunited' only in 1949 by an act of annulment of the Union of Uzhhorod (1646). Two years before, in November 1947, the local bishop, Theodore Romzha, had been murdered under mysterious circumstances.[13] The Uniate eparchy of Pryashiv (Prešov) in Czechoslovakia followed suit. In April 1950 a 'popular-ecclesiastic' convention terminated the Union with Rome, using the same methods of conversion that were practised in the Western Ukraine.[14] Thus ended, by a political fiat, the 350-year-old Union of the Eastern and Roman Churches in the Ukrainian lands.[15]

What was the role of the nationality factor in the incorporation of the Ukrainian Greek Catholics into the Russian Orthodox Church? In their propaganda, promoters of the 'reunion' have accused the Uniate Church of being Polish-inspired, and of not serving the interests of the Ukrainian people but only of the ruling nations – Poland, Austria, Hungary. Later it was argued that the Church was a tool of other foreign interests, particularly those of the Vatican, with its 'Anti-Communist crusade', and of Nazi Germany. The Uniate clergy and hierarchy, it was charged, had betrayed the cause of the Eastern Slavs and become the bulwark of Roman Catholic expansion against Russia, and also against Orthodox Ukrainians and Byelorussians.[16] In particular, the Uniate Church was accused of making common cause with the Ukrainian nationalists, who in the course of World War II found themselves on the German side fighting the re-establishment of Soviet power in the Ukraine.

On the other hand, noting the national character of the Church in the Ukraine, the authors of the 'reunion' decided to respect, at least temporarily, the ethnic characteristics of the Church in the Western Ukraine, and abstained from making substantive changes in the rituals and local customs. The Ukrainian version of the

Slavonic language was kept in the liturgy; typical Uniate ceremonies and rituals remained initially untouched; a Ukrainian-language Orthodox monthly was published, etc. Only in 1950 did the Orthodox Archbishop of Lviv, Makary Oksiyuk, initiate the process of 'orthodoxisation' (*opravoslavlennya*) of former Uniates by issuing, with other West Ukrainian bishops, a pastoral letter which listed 'sixteen points to be implemented by the converted priests. The points referred to certain liturgical practices considered to be the result of Latin Rite influence. These were to be eliminated from church usage.[17]

The clergy, particularly those of local origin, were kept in the Western *oblasti* in order to maintain the appearance of continuity and of the national character of the Orthodox Church in the Ukraine. Two former Uniate priests, members of the Action Group, Antoniy Pelvetsky and Mykhaylo Melnyk, were appointed bishops of Stanyslaviv and Sambir-Drohobych eparchies respectively. The Lviv archeparchy obtained a native, West Ukrainian hierarch only in 1960 in the person of Hryhorii Zakalyak, now Archbishop of Uzhhorod. Such considerations did not apply to the eparchies of the Eastern Ukraine where Russification had already made strong inroads.

THE UNDERGROUND CHURCH

The Synod of Lviv did not solve the problem of the Uniates. The 'reunion with the Mother Church' was merely a formal act, enforced by the police apparatus, which did not succeed in totally destroying the Ukrainian Uniate Church. The Church continues to exist under the most strenuous conditions, as an illegal community, permanently exposed to persecutions and reprisals. Its members are now dispersed all over the Soviet Union. They may live in Siberia as forced settlers, after having spent many years of exile in the labour camps; thousands of them live in the Eastern Ukraine, outside the traditional Uniate territory.

Only in compact communities, and mainly in remote areas, are they able to assert their commitment to the Catholic Church according to traditional religious rites. Otherwise, there is the family which, if not ethnically mixed and religiously indifferent, does continue the traditions and practices of the suppressed Church. The Uniate religion in such cases becomes somewhat analogous to the Muslim religion, i.e. not an institutionalised

Church with formal hierarchy and status, but rather a psychological attitude and national–cultural identification, with a certain set of customs and practices zealously kept. Major religious feasts are observed within the family or among close friends (Easter, Christmas Eve, religious name-days, etc.). Baptism, religious nuptial rites, and funerals are frequently performed by a Christian priest, often secretly, and some times even by a Uniate priest.

The majority of Uniates maintain the attitude that the performance of certain church functions even by Orthodox priests does not infringe on their Uniate identity and consciousness. This is particularly true if the Orthodox priest is a former Uniate who only superficially adopted the administrative jurisdiction of the Orthodox Church. In general, this seems to be the present state of mind and faith among the majority of believers in the Western Ukraine. They attend services in the same church, often have a local priest, practise virtually the same religious rites and customs, and receive the same sacraments, as they did prior to 1946. For them very little has changed. The common people even make a distinction between the parishes and priests who continue to be 'our own', and those who are exponents of the new ecclesiastical policy and accept fully Russian Orthodoxy.[18] The latter are suspect and avoided by the Uniate faithful.

It is difficult to establish how many former Uniates have totally and sincerely converted to the Orthodox Church. No statistics are available, nor could public opinion be surveyed in this respect. From casual conversation with people from the Ukraine and from reports of tourists, one can estimate that the number of such people is minimal. The majority of the faithful, i.e. those more or less practising the religion, have apparently remained Uniates at heart, as have some 'converted' priests. A certain number of parishes and priests in the late 1950s openly repudiated Orthodoxy in expectation that the Khrushchevian 'thaw' would eventually result in the restoration of the Uniate Church[19]

Moreover, there is a category of Uniates who refuse to accept Orthodoxy and who steadfastly continue to assert their commitment to Catholicism. In a few cases, mainly in West Ukrainian cities where some Latin Rite churches and priests are still active, they are satisfying their religious needs by attending those churches. There were 132 Roman Catholic parishes in 1961 in the Ukraine.[20] Visitors to Lviv report that services in the Roman Catholic cathedral are attended by many Uniates. The genuine 'recalcitrants' depend on the services of 'true' Uniate priests, i.e. those who did not pass to Russian Orthodoxy. Such priests are active, although it is difficult to establish their number. A figure of 200 to 300 now residing in Western *oblasti* would be a conservative guess.[21]

The émigré press frequently publishes the obituaries of priests in the Ukraine, most of whom remained Catholics to the end. In 1955–56 many Uniate priests returned from exile, having survived ten to twelve years' imprisonment. Although some were physically broken, they continued religious services in private. There was also a certain number of priests, monks and nuns who did not sign the act of subjection to the Orthodox Church, and who formally declared themselves as having left the religious life. If not arrested, they continued to perform certain religious functions, such as baptism, confession, liturgical services, funerals, etc., and even offered religious instruction to minors.[22]

The Soviet press reported the existence of theological courses for those aspiring to the priesthood in the Uniate Church.[23] The religious communities, both male and female, also continue their precarious existence and maintain novitiates. Employed in various professions, nuns and monks live in small groups according to monastic rules. They conduct services in private homes, take care of their co-religionists, and are active in charitable work. All the pre-war religious orders and congregations are known to have members. These include the Basilians, Studites, Redemptorists, and, among the female communities, Basilian Sisters, Servants of Immaculate Mary, St Vincent's Sisters, Josephite Sisters, etc.[24]

In the countryside, the religious life of the Uniates is less suppressed. Local authorities occasionally tolerate services in abandoned churches and chapels, which do not have an Orthodox priest and have not been converted into storage quarters. In cases where a priest is not available on Sundays and holidays, the people gather in private homes or in the woods to celebrate matins or vespers, a practice which is permissible according to the church rules. The figure of the travelling Uniate priest going from one village to another is an integral part of the national landscape in the Western Ukraine. In addition, many people are participating in religious services by listening every Sunday to the Vatican

Radio broadcast of liturgy in the Ukrainian–Byzantine Rite, as well as to other religious programmes.

In 1968–69, during a campaign of reprisals against the active priests, at least two dozen names of 'recalcitrants' became known through the Soviet press and from Ukrainian or Russian *samizdat* publications. Their homes were searched, and religious books, vestments and money confiscated. Many were arrested, beaten and then released; others were tried and fined or jailed.[25]

In the autumn of 1968 authorities began a new campaign of closing and transforming certain churches which remained vacant (without priests) into storage places for corn. However, at night the peasants would throw out the stored goods and clean up for Sunday services. In one case, peasants in the village of Mylyatyn decided to protest by not going to work on the collective farm. The strike lasted three days and, finally, the church was saved, although the organisers were fined thirty to fifty roubles each, for 'participating in a religious strike and for opposition to authorities'. A more dramatic event took place in Tysmenytsya in the Ivano-Frankivsk *oblast*. The church was to be demolished, but the people saved it by locking themselves inside prior to the arrival of the demolition crew. They did not leave for several days. Again there were trials as a consequence of this act of religious resistance.[26]

The most revealing event in recent years was the arrest and trial of Bishop Vasyl Velychkovsky.[27] A former Redemptorist abbot, Velychkovsky was condemned to death in 1946, but his sentence then was commuted to ten years' imprisonment. He was released from a Vorkuta camp and has lived in Lviv since 1956. Velychkovsky was secretly consecrated bishop by the Metropolitan Josyf Slipyj, when the latter was still in the U.S.S.R. In the 1960s, there was some evidence that he was co-ordinating the activities of the underground Church. In January 1969 Bishop Velychkovsky was arrested and tried for alleged contacts with Uniate centres abroad, for listening to Vatican broadcasts and for anti-Soviet sermons. According to the Soviet press, he had written a religious book on the miraculous ikon of the Mother of God of Perpetual Help, which contained 'many slanders against the Soviet state'. 'He also attempted', the reports continue, 'to prove that Uniate priests are Ukrainian patriots . . .'.[28] After completing his three-year sentence in a prison in the Donetsk region, the Soviet authorities released Velychkovsky and ordered him to leave the country.[29]

Radical groups among the Uniates assert their opposition to the Soviet religious policy more openly. The Soviet press in the Ukraine occasionally reports on the Uniate group called *Pokutnyky* (Penitents), whose members resort to typical methods of secret sects. They assemble at night in private homes for prayer, religious singing and preaching. They defy the authorities by advocating a negative attitude towards public life and indifference to the economic programmes of the Government. According to their teaching, the Ukrainian people must repent their sins of the past in order to be delivered from their present yoke. The existence of the *Pokutnyky* movement and its fanatical attachment to certain cults (the pilgrimages to the place of 'apparition' of the Holy Virgin in Serednya, the insistence on strict preservation of all the feast days, fasting, etc.) have been pointed out in a recent Soviet publication on religious matters:

> The most strikingly anti-social and anti-Soviet form of intertwining religion and nationalism is the 'Neo-Uniate faith', the so-called *Pokutnyky* movement which found a certain number of followers in the Western *oblasti* of the Ukraine. On the one hand, the Neo-Uniates declare themselves as a purely religious group, a 'genuinely apostolic faith'; on the other hand, they are playing on national feelings by asserting that the Ukraine which 'has been oppressed in captivity and serfdom for long centuries' is being now 'resurrected by God'. Thus, they try to foment hatred of other peoples, primarily of the Russian nation which, allegedly, introduced atheism in the Ukraine. Although the *Pokutnyky* are not widely spread, this, none the less, means that, under particular conditions, there is a possibility of close interaction between religion and nationalism.[30]

Along similar lines, yet in another Uniate milieu, a trend towards a new ideological orientation of Ukrainian Catholicism has been observed. Its existence was confirmed by a Soviet author who, in a book on atheism, wrote about Uniate initiatives 'to establish a Church of Kievan-Christian tradition which would have Orthodox rituals and Catholic dogmas'.[31]

The Soviet press reported 'a marked intensification of the

activities of the former Uniate clergy in separate *oblasti* of the Ukraine in recent times' and their 'illegal agitation' for the re-establishment of the Uniate Church.[32] On a number of occasions, Uniate believers attempted to legalise their Church by petitioning the Soviet authorities to register Uniate parish congregations, according to existing regulations.[33] However, all their requests were refused without explanation.

A Soviet Russian author, in a book on the Catholic Church, also refers to such initiatives on the part of former Uniates in the Ukraine:

> The propaganda of ideas and decisions of Vatican II by the foreign press and radio which is, in one form or another, designed for the Soviet Union, has inspired certain Uniate churchmen. They are spreading among the people, and in particular among the former Uniate faithful who returned to the Orthodox Church, diverse rumours; they slander Soviet reality, inspire letters to various Soviet authorities with demands to restore the Greek Catholic Church in the Ukraine.[34]

The Russian dissidents also acknowledged intensification of religious resistance among Ukrainian Uniates. *The Chronicle of Current Events* reported in 1969 that 'the Eastern Rite Church has become more active in recent years, and the number of its priests detained and beaten up by the police has grown'.[35]

THE RUSSIAN ORTHODOX CHURCH VERSUS UKRAINIAN UNIATES

There can be no doubt that the leaders of the Russian Orthodox Church willingly collaborated with the Soviet Government in the continuous suppression of the Uniate Church. This collaboration was not affected by the fact that the Russian Church, too, became the target of Soviet anti-religious policy. The Uniates in the Western Ukraine, however, were found more dangerous from a political point of view than the Orthodox Church; hence the support given by the regime to the Orthodox leadership in 're-uniting' West Ukrainians.

The Russian Orthodox hierarchy never achieved the desired results in the 'Orthodoxisation' (*opravoslavlennya*) of the Western Ukraine. It had to satisfy itself, at least temporarily, with the formal recognition of the supremacy of the Moscow Patriarchate, as well as with the administrative banning of the Uniate church organisation. Marginal activities of a handful of Uniate priests could be tolerated. However, when such activities became a visible threat to the position of the Orthodox Church in the Ukraine, the Orthodox bishops and clergy began a new struggle against the 'remnants' of the Uniates. In 1968–69, the problem became more serious when news penetrated from neighbouring Czechoslovakia about the restoration of the Uniate Church under the impact of the 'Czech spring'.[36]

This coincided with attempts to legalise the Uniate Church in the U.S.S.R. The unwanted consequences of an eventual restoration of the Eastern Catholic Church were realised by both the Russian Church and the Soviet authorities, and they felt compelled to move vigorously against such attempts. The Government feared the national character of such a Church, and the Orthodox leadership recognised that a Catholic Church with Eastern rites might be attractive to some Orthodox elements disillusioned by the opportunist policy of the Moscow Patriarchate *vis-à-vis* the Communist State.

Consequently, new reprisals against the Uniates began in the autumn of 1968 after the invasion of Czechoslovakia. *Samizdat* sources attribute the initiative for this action to the Kiev Metropolitan Filaret (Denysenko). In 1968 a conference of the Orthodox deans and clergy from the Western Ukraine was held at the monastery of Pochaiv (Volhynia region). At this assembly complaints were raised by some Orthodox priests that the illegal Uniate activities constituted a serious obstacle in discharging their duties, and obstructed the consolidation of Orthodoxy in the Western Ukraine. The Metropolitan promised to request the Soviet Ukrainian authorities to intensify repressive measures against the Uniates. The underground source observes: 'On the basis of this request, instructions were issued by the Procuracy organs that the remnants of the Greek Catholic Church be liquidated before the centenary of Lenin's birth (1970), and thus the Russian Church may be freed from this competition.'[37]

To counteract the influence and popularity of the Uniate Church both at home and abroad, the Orthodox hierarchy intensified their anti-Uniate propaganda. The anniversaries of the liquidation of the Unions of Brest (25th) and of Uzhhorod (20th) were commemorated in the Ukraine with grand éclat. In May

1971 celebrations took place in the city of Lviv with seven Ukrainian bishops, headed by Filaret, the Exarch of the Ukraine, in attendance. The patriarchal *locum tenens,* Metropolitan Pimen, praised the 'reunion' in a special message. Filaret, in his speech, labelled the Uniate Church as 'anti-people and an alien factor' in Ukrainian life and history. 'Instead of church unity', said Filaret, 'it has brought us divisions, hostility and hatred. It suppressed the religious and national self-consciousness of our people . . .'. Moreover, the Union was denounced from the ecumenical point of view. The Kiev Metropolitan stated that the Union of Brest was 'a violation of Christian conscience and it did not serve the unity of faith, but the unity of external organisation and the power of the Roman Church'.[38] None the less, Filaret had to admit that the Lviv Synod of 1946 was made possible 'as a result of Soviet victory in World War II and the liberation of the Western Ukraine'.[39]

Similar arguments and ideological rationalisation for the liquidation of the Uniate Church were presented by Filaret at the Zagorsk *Sobor* two weeks later. Here the Exarch of the Ukraine also expressed the need for a cautious treatment of the 'reunited' Ukrainians, and characterised the religious situation in the Western Ukraine as follows:

> Much has been done by bishops and priests in overcoming the consequences of the Union and in strengthening the Orthodox consciousness. . . . Yet we should not forget that, in the course of 350 years, the Union has left a definite impact on the religious consciousness, as well as on the rituals. The hierarchy and the clergy ought to continue thoughtful efforts to overcome the consequences of the Union, attentively respecting the local church customs which do not contradict the Orthodox faith and teachings.[40]

Among its decisions, the Zagorsk *Sobor* adopted a resolution concerning the dissolved Union of the Ukrainian Church with Rome which read:

> The *Sobor* marks, as a notable event in the life of the Russian Orthodox Church, the return to Orthodoxy in 1946 and 1949 of Greek Catholics in Galicia and Transcarpathia, as well as the annulment of the Brest and Uzhhorod Unions, which in their times were imposed by force.[41]

Filaret's speeches and the *Sobor* resolution set the tone for other official statements by the spokesmen of the R.O.C. Recently the Archbishop of Lviv, Nikolai, gave an interview to a Ukrainian-language Communist weekly in New York. Nikolai's statement, a highly polemical document, was directed against the Ukrainian Catholic hierarchy abroad, headed by Archbishop Major Josyf Slipyj, which had marked the 375th anniversary of the Brest Union by issuing a joint pastoral letter in Rome in October 1971.[42]

Reaction to the continuing existence of the Ukrainian Catholic and Orthodox Churches outside of the Soviet sphere of control, and to the increased interest in them among the Soviet Ukrainian population, is not expressed only in polemics, invectives and reprisals.[43] Both the Moscow Patriarchate and the Soviet regime are trying to neutralise the influence of the Ukrainian churches abroad by granting certain concessions to the national sentiments of Ukrainian believers. In the West Ukrainian eparchies and parishes, the Ukrainian version of Church-Slavonic is still in liturgical use, and the sermons are mostly preached in Ukrainian. Former Uniates are allowed to maintain certain rituals, forms of ecclesiastic vestments and decors, local customs, religious songs and music, all displaying more local characteristics. The ecclesiastical authorities in Moscow and Kiev caution their subordinates against hasty 'Orthodoxisation'.[44]

In the last few years, other limited concessions have been granted to Ukrainians which, at least on the surface, play down the prevailing Russian character of the R.O.C. in the Ukraine. Those concessions, far from being a genuine Ukrainianisation and autonomisation, are manifested in the following measures.

1. The formal status of the Ukrainian Exarchate, the only one existing in the U.S.S.R., has been somewhat upgraded.[45] For the first time a native Ukrainian was named the Exarch in 1966, Filaret Denysenko.
2. The hierarchy in the Ukraine now consists predominantly of ethnic Ukrainians (14 out of 16 bishops). This was not the case in the 1940s and 1950s. A number of native Ukrainians serve as bishops in other parts of the U.S.S.R., and even abroad. In the ranks of the hierarchy in the Ukraine there are presently three former Uniates: Nikolai Yuryk of Lviv-Ternopil (promoted in 1971 to the rank

of Metropolitan), Yosyf Savrash of Ivano-Frankivsk, and Hryhorii Zakalyak of Uzhhorod-Mukachiv.

3. Recently, a greater role was assigned to Kiev for activities outside the U.S.S.R. In December 1969 a Ukrainian branch of the Patriarchate's Department of External Ecclesiastical Relations was established in Kiev.[46] A vicar of the Kievan Metropolitan, Bishop Makariy Svystun, was placed in charge of all patriarchal parishes in Canada and the United States.

4. In 1968 the publication of the Ukrainian Orthodox monthly *Pravoslavny visnyk* was resumed (having started in Lviv in 1946,[47] but suspended in 1963). Initially intended only for Western Ukrainian eparchies, the monthly was later made into the official publication of the Ukrainian Exarchate with the editorial offices transferred to Kiev. For the first time since the 1920s, an Orthodox prayer book was published in 1968 in Ukrainian and the Ukrainian rendition of Church-Slavonic. There is also a modest annual edition of the Church Calendar in Ukrainian.

During the last few years the Soviet Government and Moscow Patriarchate have followed closely and with some concern certain activities in the Ukrainian churches abroad. These include efforts by the Ukrainian Catholics to establish their own Patriarchate (of Kiev-Halych) within the Catholic Church, and a parallel movement among the Ukrainian Orthodox to consolidate their several jurisdictions into the single Ukrainian Orthodox Autocephalous Church.[48] Not surprisingly, the Ukrainian problem has prominently figured in Moscow's recent diplomatic and ecumenical contacts with the Holy See, and in its relations with the Ecumenical Patriarchate of Constantinople. For the improvement of Soviet-Vatican relations, and expanded ecumenical dialogue, in which the Roman Curia is strongly interested, Moscow presents a high price: recognition of the *fait accompli* of the liquidation of the Uniate Church in the Ukraine: less stress on the existence of the Ukrainian Catholic Church in the West; and cessation of any support for the Ukranian religious and national aspirations. There are, apparently, influential circles in the Vatican which attentively follow such suggestions and overtures.[49]

At the same time both the Moscow Patriarchate and the Soviet anti-religious press have been attacking the Ukrainian Autocephalous Orthodox Church – its past activities in the Ukraine and its continued existence abroad. One of the most recent attacks appeared in the well publicised message of March 1972, addressed by Patriarch Pimen of Moscow to the Ecumenical Patriarch, attempting to dissuade Constantinople from any contacts with this 'schismatic' and 'chauvinistic' Church.[50]

Despite a continuing propaganda barrage against the two Ukrainian national churches,[51] there have been many indications of a rising interest in the Ukrainian religious heritage among the Ukrainian intelligentsia and youth. In the face of intensified denationalisation pressures, the young creative intelligentsia, in particular, has shown an increasing awareness of the close, intimate links between traditional religion, native culture and nationality. Hence their revived interest in theology and liturgy, religious tradition and customs, and church music, art and architecture. It appears that the present Ukrainian generation is anxious to preserve these values as part of their national heritage. Consequently it is not surprising that the government-sponsored Society for the Protection of Historical Monuments has found a genuine response among many people, since, through it, they attempt to preserve some old churches, ikons and other religious artistic objects.[52]

Some young artists and literati in the contemporary Ukraine are religiously inspired in the most genuine way. The woodcuts of Borys Soroka revive Ukrainian pre-Christian mythology, as well as biblical themes. A young poet, Ihor Kalynets, pours directly from the foundation of religious imagery and resounds like a real Christian bard preaching evangelical virtues, sacrifice and piety.[53]

This national-religious awareness of the intelligentsia helps to explain the tremendous popularity of the officially published novel *Sobor* (The Cathedral) by a leading Ukrainian Soviet novelist, Oles Honchar. The novel – 100,000 copies were printed – was belatedly criticised, and as a result its second printing was confiscated and destroyed.[54] In this work, Honchar sings an ode to a Baroque Cossack cathedral standing for the Ukraine's national past and for her present national distinctiveness. It is a symbol of the permanence and survival of the Ukrainian nation. Honchar's

novel castigates the bureaucrats and 'poachers' of national monuments, anxious to destroy the cathedral. 'Guard the cathedrals of
your souls, friends. Yes, the cathedrals of your souls!', exclaims
one of the characters of the novel to his contemporaries and to
the future generations.

This close linkage between national culture and religious
tradition was dramatised by a leading Ukrainian dissident intel-
lectual, Valentyn Moroz, in his essay 'The Chronicle of Resistance'.
Writing about the Uniate Church in the Western Ukraine, Moroz
summed up the new awareness of the young Ukrainian intelligentsia:

> . . . the most convenient way of destroying foundations of a
> nation is to employ the pretext of fighting against the Church.
> The Church has grown into cultural life so deeply that it is
> impossible to touch it without damaging the spiritual struc-
> ture of the nation. It is impossible to imagine traditional
> values without the Church. Finally, one must understand that
> the struggle against the Church means a struggle against the
> culture.[55]

NOTES

1. Ukrainian Catholics or Uniates were rarely referred to simply as Catholics;
   they were called Greek Catholics or, at the present time, Ukrainian Catholics,
   somewhat separate from other Catholics in their own mind, and in the
   popular opinion of their non-Ukrainian co-religionists.
2. Asked about their nationality, the people often identified themselves as being
   Orthodox or Uniates or, when asked about their religion, they would answer
   as being of the 'Ruthenian faith' (*Ruska vira*).
3. M. Hrushevsky, *Z istorii relihiynoi dumky na Ukraini* (From the History of Religious
   Thought in the Ukraine) (Lviv, 1925); V. Lypynsky, *Relihiya i Tserkva v
   istorii Ukrainy* (Religion and the Church in the History of the Ukraine)
   (Philadelphia, 1925).
4. This is recognised even by such critics of Ukrainian and Byelorussian Autocephaly as Harvey Fireside, *Icon and Swastika. The Russian Orthodox Church
   under Nazi and Soviet Control* (Cambridge, Mass., 1971).
5. For the historical treatment of the Union of Brest (1596) and of the Uniate
   Church, see *Ukraine: A Concise Encyclopaedia* (Toronto, 1971), Vol. II. This
   writer presented his critical assessment of the Union and its aftermath for
   Ukrainian religious and political developments in a recent article 'Beresteyska
   Uniya z suchasnoi perspektyvy' (The Union of Brest from a Contemporary
   Perspective), *Ukrainsky Samostiinyk* (Munich), Nos 10, 11, October, Nos 11,
   12, November–December 1972.
6. 'Khronika oporu' of V. Moroz was published abroad in many Ukrainian
   periodicals, among others, *Ukrainsky Samostiinyk*, October 1970 (translation
   mine). English edition: *Chronicle of Resistance in Ukraine* (Baltimore, 1970).

7. According to Moroz: 'In the conditions of Eastern Europe, the Church was the only force independent of authorities. Let us take the Ukrainian renaissance in Galicia. What a miserable role the teacher played here in comparison to that of the priest! The teacher was a state employee; he trembled in order not to be dismissed from his work. A priest did not share this fear. The majority of the Ukrainian cultural leaders came from a priestly background. The priest was often and justly criticised, but it must not be forgotten that he was the one on whose shoulders the Ukrainian movement rested. It should be clearly stated that it was the Ukrainian Church which constituted the barrier against Polonization in Galicia' (*ibid.*).

8. The fullest, though not necessarily sympathetic Western treatment of Ukrainian Autocephaly, appears in F. Heyer, *Die Orthodoxe Kirche in der Ukraine von 1917 bis 1945* (Köln-Braunsfeld, 1953).

9. Until recently, the official name of this Church was the 'Greek Catholic Church' and this name is still used in the Ukraine. In the 1950s, the Uniates abroad began to use the name 'The Ukrainian Catholic Church', a practice to which the Vatican also adheres.

10. On the fate of the Uniate Church after 1945 see *First Victims of Communism* (Rome, 1953); I. Hrynioch, 'The Destruction of the Ukrainian Catholic Church in the Soviet Union', *Prologue* (New York), Vol. IV (1960), pp. 5–51; and B. Bociurkiw, 'The Uniate Church in the Soviet Ukraine: A Case Study in Soviet Church Policy', *Canadian Slavonic Papers*, Vol. VII (1965), pp. 89–113.

11. For the official Synod proceedings, see *Diyannia Soboru Hreko-Katolytskoi Tserkvy u Lvovi 8–10. III. 1946* (Lviv, 1946).

12. Metropolitan Josyf Slipyj (tried several times) spent 18 years in prison and labour camps, was liberated in 1963, and now lives in Rome; he is the only surviving member of the war-time Uniate hierarchy in the Ukraine; Bishop Hryhoriy Khomyshyn of Stanyslaviv (died in 1948 in prison); Bishop-auxiliary Ivan Lyatyshevsky of Stanyslaviv (spent 10 years in a concentration camp, died in 1957); Bishop Yosafat Kotsylovsky of Peremyshl (died in prison in 1947); Bishop-auxiliary Hryhoriy Lakota of Peremyshl (died in labour camp in 1950); Bishop-auxiliary Nykyta Budka of Lviv (died in labour camp in 1949); Bishop Mykola Charnetsky, Exarch of Volhynia (died after 10 years' imprisonment, in 1959); Monsignor Petro Werhun, Apostolic Administrator for Ukrainians in Germany (died in Siberia in 1957).

13. R. N. 'Holhota Unii v Karpatskii Ukraini' (Golgotha of the Union in the Carpatho-Ukraine), *Zhyttya i slovo* (Innsbruck), Vol. 3–4 (1948–49), pp. 327–46 (an eye-witness report).

14. Bishop Pavlo Goidych was arrested in 1950, condemned to life imprisonment, and died in prison in 1960. His Auxiliary, Vasyl Hopko, was arrested at the same time and held without trial in prison until 1967. He is now residing in Pryashiv (Prešov), pursuing his archpastoral duties but has not been entrusted by the Vatican with the administration of the rehabilitated Greek Catholic Church of Czechoslovakia. See J. Kubinyi, *The History of Prjašiv Eparchy* (Rome, 1970); *The Tragedy of the Greek-Catholic Church in Czechoslovakia* (New York, 1971).

15. The Uniate Church in Eastern Europe was preserved only in Yugoslavia (Ruthenian–Ukrainian and Croatian faithful, numbering 50,000), Hungary (mostly Hungarians and partly Magyarised Ruthenians, 200,000), and in Bulgaria (20,000 Uniate Bulgarians). In Poland the Uniate Church is tolerated, but is not recognised by the authorities and has no hierarchy of its own. There now are approximately 200–300,000 Ukrainian Uniates in Poland. This is due either to the fact that Soviet influence on the religious policies of these countries was not total, or that these religious minorities were politically

insignificant. In Romania, however, the Uniate Church, numbering over 1,500,000 (among them some 20–25,000 Ukrainians) was forcefully 'reunited' in 1948 with the Romanian Orthodox Church.

16. Particularly attacked were the activities of the late Metropolitan Sheptytsky: his interest in the Slavic East prior to and during World War I, his creation of the Russian Catholic Exarchate, and his contacts with Byelorussians, as well as with the Ukrainian Orthodox leaders. See the pamphlet by V. Rosovych (Ya. Halan), *Ƶ khrestom chy nozhem* (With a Cross or a Knife?) (Lviv, 1946).

17. *Pravoslavny visnyk*, No. 8 (1968), a jubilee article by Archbishop Nikolai of Lviv, p. 17; see also B. R. Bociurkiw, 'The Orthodox Church and the Soviet Regime in the Ukraine, 1953–1971', *Canadian Slavonic Papers*, Vol. XIV, No. 2 (1972), pp. 191–211.

18. In a few West Ukrainian cities special 'Russian parishes' were open for believers who came there from Russia (Bociurkiw, *loc. cit.*, p. 198).

19. *Ibid.*, p. 199.

20. *Ukrainska Radyanska Entsyklopediya*, Vol. VI (Kiev, 1961), p. 253.

21. A. Montonati, 'Il Cristo Distrutto dei Cattolici Ucraini', *Famiglia Cristiana* (16 April 1972), gives the figure of 300 individuals who joined the priesthood and religious orders *after* 1946.

22. According to underground reports published abroad, a priest in the village of Yaremche was sentenced in 1968 to two years' prison for teaching children catechism. The *samizdat* journal, *Ukrainsky visnyk*, Vol. I–II (Paris, 1971) and Vol. III (Winnipeg, 1971) covers the resistance of Uniates and Soviet reprisals in the Ukraine. See also 'Die Ukrainische Kirche lebt. Ein Dokument aus der Verfolgung', *Der Fels* (Regensburg), No. 5 (1972), pp. 146–9.

23. *Lvovskaya pravda*, reporting on the trial of Bishop Velychkovsky in January 1969, mentioned that he helped set up such training in the city of Ternopil. Cf. *Tserkovny Kalendar* (Chicago, 1971), p. 151. Another priest, Fr Bakhtalovsky from Kolomyya, was tried in October 1969 for secretly giving lectures in theology to a group of people. Cf. *Der Fels, loc. cit.*

24. Information on the situation of religious orders is based on the reports of recent visitors to the Ukraine.

25. This happened in villages of the Horodok *rayon* to the Uniate priests Roman Choliy, Petro Horodetsky and Petro Pyrizhok. Cf. *Ukrainsky visnyk*, Vol. I–II, *loc. cit.* and *Der Fels, loc. cit.*

26. The village blacksmith Vasyl Vasylyk was sentenced to seven years in a labour camp, and another peasant Dzyurban to five years. The indictment cited Article 62 of the Penal Code of the Ukrainian S.S.R. (anti-Soviet agitation). Cf. *Ukrainsky visnyk* and *Der Fels, loc. cit.*

27. Velychkovsky is one of several secretly consecrated Uniate bishops in the Ukraine. Their names are publicised neither by the Soviet press, nor by Uniate sources. However, their existence can be proven by reports of priestly ordinations.

28. *Vilna Ukraina* (Lviv), 14 December 1969.

29 Velychkovsky was first sent to Yugoslavia, and since the end of February 1972 he has resided in Rome. Western news agencies and press took notice of his release, and in February 1972 reported more or less correctly on his life and activities. Official Vatican sources were silent on his identity as a bishop, and referred to him only as 'Father Velychkovsky'. He settled in Canada in July 1972 with the title of 'Bishop of Lutsk', and died on 30 June 1973.

30. V. L. Bodnar, 'Osobennosti razvitiya ateizma v protsesse kulturnoi revolyutsii v natsionalnoi respublike (na materialakh zapadnykh oblastei USSR')' (The Specifics of the Development of Atheism in the Process of Cultural Revolu-

tion in a Union Republic [Based on the materials from the Western Oblasti of the Ukrainian S.S.R.]) in *Ateizm i sotsialisticheskaya kultura* (Atheism and Socialist Culture) (Moscow 1971), pp. 37–52. See also B. R. Bociurkiw, *loc. cit.*; *Ukrainsky visnyk*, Vol. III., *loc. cit.*, stresses the 'increasing influence of this group in the Western Ukraine', and attributes to it 'not only religious but also national opposition character'.

31. It is noteworthy that a similar ideological trend exists among Uniates abroad.
32. B. Bychatin and O. Suhak, 'Pered sudom istorii. Uniya-yakoyu vona ye' (Before the Court of History: Union as It Is), *Robitnycha hazeta* (Kiev), 15 March 1973.
33. In villages of Mokhany of Horodok *raion*, Khorosnytsya of Mostyska *rayon*, and others. Cf. *Der Fels, loc. cit.*
34. M. P. Mchedlov, *Katolitsizm* (Catholicism) (Moscow, 1970), p. 243. The author denounced the Pope's pronouncements, during his Fatima pilgrimage, on the 'Church of silence' which 'are nourishing the Uniates' activity'. He also attacks Cardinal Slipyj and the émigrés: 'It is not accidental that the attempts to artificially restore the Greek Uniate Church in the Ukraine and to consolidate its organisation, as well as to unite Ukrainian ecclesiastical entities, received support from both the Ukrainian counter-revolutionary clergy in exile, and from the lay bourgeois nationalists' (p. 245).
35. *U. S. News and World Reports*, 5 June 1972.
36. The Western press suggested that one of the Soviet motives for invading Czechoslovakia and cutting short the Prague experiment in democratic socialism was the fear of repercussions in the neighbouring Ukraine. On the religious front there was a rapid revival of the Eastern Rite Catholic Church in Slovakia, a tempting example for Uniates in the Ukraine. 204 out of the 240 'converted' Orthodox parishes opted in 1968–69 for Uniatism. Also, the Uniate hierarchy was re-established, and is tolerated even now, in what is one of the few vestiges of the 1968 liberalisation.
37. *Der Fels, loc. cit.* The same source mentions another measure taken by the Orthodox hierarchy: the dismissal of certain unreliable priests from among the former Uniates.
38. *Pravoslavny visnyk*, No. 7 (1971), p. 10.
39. *Ibid.*, p. 13.
40. *Zhurnal Moskovskoi Patriarkhii*, No. 8 (1971), pp. 7–14.
41. *Ibid.*, No. 6 (1971), p. 3.
42. *Ukrainski Visti* (New York), March 30, 1972. Nikolai characterised the Rome jubilee observances and the pastoral letter as 'a falsification of the situation of the Church and the people in the Ukraine'. 'Its authors', said the Orthodox prelate, 'aim to sow national animosity among brotherly nations of the Soviet Union, especially between the Ukrainian and Russian peoples'.
43. One of the critics, a Uniate priest, H. Budzynovsky (arrested in 1969), argues against the Russian character of the Orthodox Church in the Ukraine as follows: 'The Orthodox Church does not exist as a whole, but as separate Churches: Russian, Georgian, Armenian, Polish, Czechoslovak, etc. However, in fact, there is no Ukrainian Orthodox Church [in the Soviet sphere of influence. – V.M.]. In the Ukraine, the Russian Church is dominating with all the consequences following thereof. The Ukrainian language is prohibited [in the church] like in the times of the Romanovs . . . . Those were not true Orthodox people who forced others to accept Russian religion, but actually the protagonists of the godless sect of militant atheism. It is an undeniable fact that the Russian Church ceased to be an authentic Orthodox Church and turned into an atheistic-Orthodox one. . . .' See *Ukrainsky visnyk*, Vol.

I–II, *loc. cit.* Dissatisfaction with the Soviet religious policy also is felt by certain Orthodox quarters in the Ukraine. In January 1972 an Orthodox priest, Vasyl Romanyuk from Kosmach, was arrested. He wrote a letter in defence of dissident V. Moroz to the Supreme Soviet of the Ukrainian S.S.R.

44. *Pravoslavny visnyk*, No. 7 (1971), p. 12.

45. The status of the Ukrainian Exarchate (established in 1921) is not constitutionally defined as that of an autonomous Church. It is rather an honorific title due to traditional privileges of the Kiev Metropoly. Ukrainian eparchies are directly ruled by the Synod in Moscow. *Mutatis mutandis*, its status is reminiscent of the Soviet statehood of the Ukrainian S.S.R.

46. B. R. Bociurkiw, *loc. cit.*, pp. 209–10.

47. From January 1946 to January 1948 the publication was entitled *Eparkhiyalny visnyk.*

48. Filaret devoted considerable attention in his speech at the Zagorsk *Sobor* to both Ukrainian Churches. See *Zhurnal Moskovskoi Patriarkhii*, No. 8 (1971), pp. 7–14.

49. Both the Russian Church and the Vatican oppose, for their own reasons, the establishment of the Ukrainian Catholic Patriarchate, qualifying such aspirations as nationalist and politically inspired. Cardinal Willebrands as the head of the Roman Catholic delegation at the *Sobor* in 1971, did not object to the *Sobor*'s decision confirming the annulment of the Union of Brest which, for over twenty years, was considered by the Holy See to be an act of violence and injustice. Nikolai of Lviv labelled the idea of a Ukrainian Catholic Patriarchate as 'directed against the interest of Ukrainian people and detrimental to our beloved fatherland'. Cf. *Ukrainski visti* (New York), 30 March 1972.

50. See *Zhurnal Moskovskoi Patriarkhii*, No. 5 (1972), pp. 7–8.

51. Here is an incomplete list of titles (in English translation) of polemical books and pamphlets, published recently in the Ukraine, against the Uniate Church: *In the Shadow of St. George's Cathedral*, by V. Dobrych; *Celestial Manna*, by A. Hrabovskyi; *The Ideology of Treason and Corruption*, by A. Shysh; *Night Birds*, by V. Byelyaev; *Following the Path of Infamy and Treason*, by S. Danylenko; *The Cross and Treason*, by V. Symakovych; *When Dawns Crimsoned*, by S. Marchuk; *Indivisible Boundaries*, by M. Postnikov; *The Real Face of the Union*, by R. Dubovyk; *The Truth about the Union* (documents and materials); *An Alliance of Swastika and Trident*; *Coadjutor with the Right of Successor*. See also S. Danylenko, *Uniaty* (Moscow, 1972). A special 'documentary' film, *Since the Times History Remembers*, was produced to prove the anti-Soviet record of the Uniate Church.

52. The Society, although a public organisation, is not capable of seriously tackling its objectives; often Party considerations prevail over the historical and conservationist. Because of this, many patriotic individuals resort to personal initiatives: private collections of rare books, icons, organisation of little memorial museums, protection of the cemeteries of Ukrainian soldiers, etc.

53. Kalynets' poems which could not pass Soviet censorship were published abroad under the title *Poezii z Ukrainy* (Poetry from the Ukraine) (Brussels, 1970).

54. Three editions of *Sobor* were published abroad in Ukrainian; the novel is now also available in German and Polish translations.

55. V. Moroz, *Khronika oporu, loc. cit.*